JAN 2 9 2009

THE YEAR *of the* BOAT

THE YEAR *of the* BOAT

Beauty, Imperfection, and the Art of Doing It Yourself

LAWRENCE W. CHEEK

SASQUATCH BOOKS
SEATTLE

For Patty
who may have doubted
but never spoke of it

Printed in the United States of America
Published by Sasquatch Books
Distributed by PGW/Perseus
15 14 13 12 11 10 09 08   9 8 7 6 5 4 3 2 1

Cover photograph: © 2007 Julia Kuskin
Cover design: Rosebud Eustace
Interior design: Jessica Norton
Interior illustrations: Sarah Plein
Interior composition: Jessica Norton

Library of Congress Cataloging-in-Publication Data

Cheek, Lawrence W.
  The year of the boat : beauty, imperfection, and the art of doing it yourself /
Lawrence W. Cheek.
     p. cm.
  Includes bibliographical references.
  ISBN-13: 978-1-57061-544-3
  ISBN-10: 1-57061-544-6
  1. Sailboats. 2. Boatbuilding. I. Title.

VM351.C49 2008
623.822'3--dc22

                              2007049894

Sasquatch Books
119 South Main Street, Suite 400
Seattle, WA 98104
(206) 467-4300
www.sasquatchbooks.com
custserv@sasquatchbooks.com

Contents

CHAPTER I

DEEP BEAUTY

THERE ARE PLACES IN North America where no one thinks about boats. I come from one of them, El Paso, a city stuffed into the acute western wedge of Texas between Mexico and New Mexico. The only local body of water is the Rio Grande, which farmers have sucked down to a miserable mocha dribble by the time it reaches El Paso. A hundred miles upriver are a couple of reservoirs that technically qualify as boating destinations, but to me they've always looked as bleak as the windswept Chihuahuan Desert around them. In the seventeen years I lived in El Paso, I never met anyone who owned a boat nor, as far as I knew, dreamed of one.

A painting of a boat somehow imprinted itself on my childhood memory, however. It hung on a wall of the Club Zaragosa, a restaurant-nightclub just across the Mexican border. My parents frequently went there to eat, drink, and dance—*cerveza* was ten cents a bottle, and there was a brass orchestra on weekends that to my twelve-year-old ears sounded respectable. The painting depicted a serene lake somewhere in central Mexico. In the background was a volcano, and in the foreground a dark-skinned man stood on a small wooden pram, propelling it with a pole. There appeared to be no practical reason for the man to be in the boat—no fishing gear, no passengers, no larger boat he might be approaching as a tender. It appeared that the boatman might simply be wasting time, and I wondered why an artist had chosen to celebrate such a thing.

Today I'm wondering about the chain of events that has braided my recent adult life with a boat, and whether I may have just wasted a precious year. I'm building a boat—a modest wooden sailing dinghy that fits, barely, in my suburban Seattle garage—and I'm in trouble. I just discovered, thanks to the scrutiny of a boatbuilding friend in another suburb, that four months ago I left out a piece of its structure. A sprinkling of minor mistakes, scattered across the course of a year, appear to have mated and multiplied into swarms. Neighbors continually drop in and practically swoon over the boat's graceful lines, but all I see are mistakes and misjudgments, some cosmetic, some possibly fatal to its safe functioning. I'm depressed and discouraged. I don't know whether I'll have a respectable and usable sailboat when I finish it, or a learning experience that's too deeply flawed even to give away.

My work has been incomprehensibly slow, stumbling, often incompetent, plagued by doubt, and at the same time infected by too much pride to ask for help. I started out knowing I was fully unqualified to build a boat, but buoyed by the belief that *every* first-time boatbuilder is unqualified, by definition. Building a doghouse or a gazebo doesn't *begin* to prepare you for the complexities of a boat, nor for the emotional surf you're headed into.

Throughout the project, I've had a continuing struggle not so much with perfectionism—"perfect" was never my goal— but with finding a level of imperfection that seemed reasonable and comfortable. A boat must be built well enough to shield its occupants from an environment that will quickly kill them if they're fully exposed to it, must be able to sail efficiently and maneuver reliably from point A to point B, *and* return a tangible dividend of joy to its owner, balancing the inevitable grief it will also bring. A handmade wooden boat is an organic creation, nearly a living thing in itself, and the beauty designed and built into it has a direct correlation to its lifespan. "A wooden boat must be loved if it's to survive," wrote Jenny Bennett, a British editor who commissioned a professionally built daysailer about the size of mine, "and that's considerably more likely to happen if it's pretty to look at."

Over the last year I've done almost nothing *but* think about boats, building this one and learning to sail on bigger ones and trying to discern whether there is any deeper meaning in the process. I never expected any of this.

Early in my adult life I settled in Tucson, which would seem to be just as unlikely as my hometown of El Paso as a venue for anyone to entertain boat thoughts. The river that used to trickle through the southern Arizona desert, the Santa Cruz, literally dried up in the 1940s as agriculture and urban growth drained down the water table. The Santa Cruz riverbed today is a dry channel flanked incongruously with mesquite-and-cactus city parks and occasional homeless encampments pitched in the shade of sprawling tamarisk trees. But Arizona, land of audacious schemes, has substantial boating destinations: Lake Roosevelt, created by a dam on the Salt River northeast of Phoenix; and Lakes Havasu, Mohave, Mead, and Powell along the Colorado River. Among the urban legends I heard on arrival in Tucson was that Arizonans owned more boats per capita than residents of any other state. I swallowed it—Arizona seemed so exotic that any cultural perversity might be plausible—but this statistic, at least, turned out to be spurious. One in every thirty-four Arizonans, according to current registration figures, owns a boat. In Minnesota, one in six.

I came to know a handful of people in Arizona who had boats—wealthy folks who kept sailboats in San Diego or the Sea of Cortez, or working stiffs who would trailer their speedboats to Lake Roosevelt for grim weekends of beer and sunburn. I have one memorable boat story, which involved a friend in medical school at the University of Arizona in the early 1980s.

In October of 1983 it rained furiously and freakishly for three days in Tucson and even more in the mountains heaped like a collar around the city. The Santa Cruz and its normally dry tributaries, most notably the Rillito, suddenly reawakened as real rivers. The Rillito (ironically "Little River" in Spanish) is an eroded channel up to eight hundred feet wide, and at the peak of this flood, chocolate-brown water boiled through it so savagely that it gobbled acre-sized bites of riverbank, one after another, like a dog devouring meatloaf. I stood among a knot of saucer-eyed spectators on a hilltop and watched as one of the acre-bites collapsed into the Rillito's maw, the house on it splintering like a popsicle-stick model. At exactly this same hour Michael Collier was in a Saturday morning pediatrics lecture at the medical school, looking out at the rain and daydreaming about the kayak languishing in the shed behind his house. As soon as class ended he phoned friend Curt Green, a fellow kayaker who was typically "up for anything," and the pair lashed their kayaks to Collier's '66 Volkswagen bus and headed for a possible launch spot upstream on the Rillito.

"When we got there and saw it, our jaws dropped," Collier recalled later. "It was just awesome. It was running at 20,000 cubic feet per second. We didn't hesitate for a minute."

Collier and his friend launched into what amounted to a five-mile-long brownwater maelstrom and rode it halfway through Tucson. "We were in trains of waves that were higher than the kayak was long—twelve feet," Collier recalled. "We passed condos that were actively falling in. At one point I pulled into a nest of branches to rest, and shared it with a rattlesnake." He insisted it wasn't all that dangerous. "I'd been kayaking for twelve years at that point, and I had a bombproof roll. I'd do it again today if those skills were intact."

I thought then that Collier was certifiably insane, but he graduated from medical school, completed his internship and residency, and is today a respected practicing physician.

Conditional insanity, induced by the poorly understood reaction of water, human, and boat, is a more likely diagnosis.

It is possible that boat mania is somehow genetically encoded in the human brain. Our distant ancestors built boats to extend their foraging range and populate new lands when the natural resources at home grew scarce. Natural selection would therefore seem to favor those with the more adventurous genes. (The earliest evidence for human travel in boats is the settlement of Australia and New Guinea at least 40,000 years ago—around the time that Neanderthals, who apparently built no boats, vanished from the earth.)

If boats aren't imprinted in our atavistic makeup, it seems provably certain that the craving to visit or inhabit new environments is. And a boat—a raft made from logs, a kayak, a luxury yacht, a battleship—is the most practical way of adapting ourselves to a natural environment for which we are physiologically unsuited. Collier wasn't quite crazy enough to *swim* the raging Rillito, and if he had been, his genetic line would have terminated abruptly, right there. With the help of boats, people cheerfully accept preposterous risks or hardships to be out on the water. I recently toured a sailboat that the owners had lived on for several years. They were a family of five. The boat was twenty-seven feet long.

A substantial fraction of our wild-ass dreams involve boats in some way or another. A travel writer named Paul Bennett explained in *National Geographic Adventure* magazine how he and his wife, Lani, decided over martinis one evening in 1999 to chuck their jobs, buy a sailboat, and set off on a transoceanic voyage with no goal other than staying afloat and alive. Neither had any substantial sailing experience. But they did it, and lived to tell. Around this same time, Jerry Joslin, an Oregon bronze sculptor, noticed a seedy-looking Chinese junk docked on the Columbia River, a couple of kids living on it for cheap rent. He bought it and spent five intense years restoring it. "Sometimes we do crazy things," he told a local newspaper. "Sometimes it turns out in life you are well advised to do that; it's called chasing a dream."

In a gemlike piece titled "The Sea and the Wind That Blows" essayist E. B. White, a lifelong sailor, explained such "crazy things" with eloquent rationality: "If a man must be obsessed by something, I suppose a boat is as good as anything, perhaps a bit better than most. A small sailing craft is not only beautiful, it is seductive and full of strange promise and the hint of trouble." John Steinbeck, reflecting on a 1940 expedition in the Sea of Cortez, suggested something more mystical: "Some have said they have felt a boat shudder before she struck a rock, or cry when she beached and the surf poured into her. This is not mysticism, but identification; man, building this greatest and most personal of all tools, has in turn received a boat-shaped mind, and the boat, a man-shaped soul."

I paid little attention to boats and water through the decades I lived in Arizona. Mountains and canyons formed a more obvious and practical attraction. I never had the nerve to try climbing with ropes and carabiners, but I came to love hiking in steep, spiky places. The last of the three addresses my wife, Patty, and

I occupied in Tucson was a house at the northeastern edge of the city where the Santa Catalina Mountains spilled into the desert basin in a tumble of canyons. I was working from home by then, and I fell into a routine of hiking those canyons for two or three hours every morning before settling into the day's research and writing. I could no more envision living in an environment without mountains than one without oxygen.

In 1995, unexpectedly, we moved to Seattle. It was a career move for Patty, who was recruited into a nursing management job at a colossal hospital. There were mountains on the horizons whenever the rain and fog relented for long enough to see them, and it was no coincidence that we bought a house in the one suburb that has a halfway decent mountain right in it.

Patty had grown up in Houston, forty miles from the Gulf of Mexico, but this was the first time I had ever lived near ocean or lakes. Less than four months after moving, we got ourselves seduced by the lavishly abundant water of Washington. On a weekend trip to the San Juan Islands, we spotted a sign in the waterfront village of Eastsound: "Sea Kayak Tours—No Experience Necessary." Well, why not? Something about being on an island, even for a weekend, overwrites the default-mode inhibitions. The tether to solid ground, to mainland personal histories, is temporarily slack. An hour later, bobbing on the wavelets of Doe Bay, we knew we were having a life-altering experience. Since then we've logged thousands of kayak miles—mostly close to home in Puget Sound and British Columbian waters, but also off the coast of Maine and in Mexico's Sea of Cortez.

We felt no urge to graduate to any larger type of boat. Sea kayaking appeared to present more than enough challenge and adventure to last us the rest of our lives. A sea kayak can go anywhere, as long as one is patient enough to do it at a speed of 3 knots, and cultivating that patience (along with the physical conditioning that necessarily accompanies it) is a virtuous goal. A kayak, in fact, is not only a boat, but also an extension of the human body; the paddler morphs into a kind of honorary sea mammal. You're intimately connected with the marine environment, and you learn to appreciate it—and deeply respect it—at many different levels.

Then came a magazine assignment to do a roundup of the Northwest's wooden boat shows. We first hit the Center for Wooden Boats' July festival on Seattle's Lake Union, then the September Wooden Boat Festival in Port Townsend. Between them we saw more than two hundred watercraft of every possible description: sailboats, motor cruisers, speedboats, tugboats, rowboats, canoes, kayaks. Most of them, if not quite all, were beautiful. Their owners also shared a common quality: a devotion that bordered on fanaticism. I talked with several.

"People come aboard, shake their heads in amazement, and ask, 'How can you possibly keep up with it?'" said the skipper of a stunning seventy-eight-foot schooner named *Sugartime*, based in Honolulu. "I say, how can you *not* keep up with it? How can you ignore the responsibility of maintaining a thing of such beauty, fifty-two tons of the finest wood ever grown?"

Another owner told me he'd just cast off his Seattle dental practice because it was demanding time that his boat, a seventy-three-foot tug built in 1909 but now undergoing renovation into a pleasure cruiser, needed more urgently. "Three mangled fingers, four lost girlfriends, five lawsuits, and close to half a million dollars—and here I am," he said. "But I know people who've spent more on psychiatry and therapy than I have on this boat, and I'm a lot happier."

The owner of a 1928 salmon troller converted to cruising confirmed that a staggering amount of labor goes into rebuilding and maintaining such a boat. "There aren't too many successful conversions like this," he said. "But there are a lot of failed dreams."

I asked directly about obsession. "A wooden boat will take every bit of perfectionism you can throw at it," said the owner of a thirty-three-foot sloop. "It's real easy to get obsessive—to go overboard, so to speak. You have to constantly remind yourself to keep looking at the big picture, and quit obsessing over the flaws that only you will ever see."

I wasn't prepared for what happened next—it came out of nowhere, as unlikely as an iceberg in the Gulf of Mexico. We were studying an exquisite forty-year-old, forty-five-foot, teak-planked sloop, recently restored to within an inch of her life, with a sign offering her for sale at $189,000.

"That's how much equity we have in the house," Patty said evenly. "It's big enough we could live aboard."

Some moments back I linked boats and wild-ass dreams, but I never would have imagined my wife contriving one of the latter. She is wise, logical, prudent, impulsive only to the point of adopting a homeless cat that might show up at the door. We knew absolutely nothing about sailing, living aboard a boat, or maintaining any watercraft more complicated than a kayak. I waited for her to toss off this freak whim with a laugh, but she didn't. She was staring at the boat with a glint of steel in her eyes. The vision of owning this boat, *fusing our entire lives to it*, had started as a shiver in her spine, bypassed the Rational Judgment Department, and lodged with electric intensity in her cortex. She was boatstruck—a phenomenon that Michael Ruhlman, in his excellent chronicle *Wooden Boats*, says occurs only infrequently among women. But none of us is immune: woman, man, architect, zoologist, El Pasoan.

We humans, no matter our gender or culture, crave to be around beauty. This is another quality that seems to be genetically imprinted, and it has to do with recognizing and feeling comforted by certain recurring patterns in nature. The swirl of a spiral galaxy and the concordant curl of a nautilus shell both evoke feelings of pleasure or even awe. We see in their similarity an underlying order to the universe, which is a warming reassurance in the midst of the messy unpredictability of human society—and of my office desk, for that matter.

A wooden boat is a more plausible object of desire than most man-made creations. It's an architectural form that pays respect to nature in a direct and honest manner. Its shape is determined by the nature of its material and the need to carve as efficiently as possible through water and air. It extends roots deep into the human story, connecting cultures throughout recorded history, and before. Remnants of an Egyptian riverboat from 2600 BC and a Viking ship of AD 800 have eerily similar forms, and any five-year-old in deepest Nebraska today would recognize them both as boats. A *wooden* boat in particular forms a retort to the prevailing pattern of intentional obsolescence and throwaway cheapness that has infected practically every other thing we buy and use today, including our houses. The only reason to throw away a well-crafted wooden boat would be if the owner has let it deteriorate beyond a reasonable feasibility of repair—and when that happens, half the time some swooning fool will try an unfeasible restoration anyway.

The swooners may be giving in to an urge to connect with something more powerful than the beauty of surface and line, something that comprises the qualities of authenticity and integrity. For easy reference, I'll call this *deep beauty*, and I plan to go into it more extensively later. But briefly, an object that has it would exemplify respect for materials, so that it does not mask or distort the essential nature of its component parts. Its design would precisely fulfill the needs of its user. And its form would not only follow function, but also relate in a deeper sense to the environment where it's created and used.

How many of the things that we own might qualify? In a typical American household, practically nothing—including the house itself. Almost nothing mass-produced will fulfill all three conditions. (The classic Gem paper clip, which cannot be improved, is an exception.) Many people own beautiful antique furniture, but how well, if at all, can a Chippendale armoire adapt to the functional needs of a twenty-first-century household? If we do happen to own something whose value and usefulness actually transcends generations, we are, I believe, blessed by it. Essayist Scott Russell Sanders once described a hammer, a saw, and a framing square that his grandfather and father had used in succession, then passed on to him. The tools functioned as well as they had two generations back, because they had been built to last and the work they had to do had not changed. More importantly, Sanders had inherited the fiber of their users through them. "I was taught early on that a saw is not to be used apart from a square," Sanders recalled. "'If you're going to cut a piece of wood,' my father insisted, 'you owe it to the tree to cut it straight.'" His tools had been sharpened, permanently, with the morality of good workmanship.

The implausible success of *WoodenBoat* magazine testifies to our longing for these qualities. It's deeper than romanticism or nostalgia. When a New England boatbuilder named Jon Wilson launched the magazine in 1974, only a small, hard core of enthusiasts was thinking about—or building or restoring—wooden boats of any kind. Fiberglass, invented in the 1940s, had made the mass production of small boats possible, and the consequence was the democratization of pleasure boating. Who could argue with that? Wilson, though, believed that wooden boats still resonated with something at the heart of human culture, or even the individual human soul, something that would not become obsolete. In a retrospective five years after launching the magazine, he wrote:

> Wooden boats remind me a lot about what we've forgotten—
> or perhaps never knew. With rare exception, their shapes and
> structures reveal the accumulated experience of thousands
> of years. They have pleasing shapes, for the most part; the
> material itself demands it. As if the grace of the forest trees
> were bequeathed in abundance to every plank sewn. And each

plank, in turn, has carried with it the duty to lie gracefully in place, resisting to the end any move toward the awkward and angular. That duty was once well understood. Designers, builders, and just plain lovers of boats could respond in awe to the nature of wood and let their hearts and hands be guided by it.

WoodenBoat started with exactly two subscribers and an office that consisted of a corner in Wilson's Maine cabin, which incidentally lacked electricity, phone, and plumbing. In 2007 its paid circulation nearly touched 80,000, which is surely more than the number of functional wooden boats in the country. Organizations and museums dedicated to the revival have blossomed. There are at least two dozen annual wooden boat festivals in North America. The one at Port Townsend, which by 2007 had blossomed into a three-day weekend blowout of music, art, food, workshops, and some two hundred boats, attracts 25,000 people every year.

In some people's minds the wooden boat revival has assumed moral dimensions. A few years back, a letter to the editor in *WoodenBoat* laid it bare: "The mass production of fiberglass boats is solely responsible for the unruly and discourteous crowds that we find on the water today."

The ripe whiff of elitism wafts from that dock, and I don't share it. I've never had any antipathy toward fiberglass boats, but I've never quite felt rapture in their presence, either. At that first wooden boat show I found I loved the visual warmth of wooden boats, sailboats in particular, and also the fact that every one of them, even a simple dinghy, contained a story. At the same time, I had serious reservations about my suitability to become one of those stories. All my life I've enjoyed building things, but I hate maintaining *anything*. I avoid gardening, fence painting, window washing, gutter cleaning, furnace filter replacing, and most other essential chores associated with home ownership. I run the "spring cleaning" program on my computer once every three or four springs, and clean out the obsolete accumulations in my filing cabinets only when the drawers refuse to accept another scrap of paper. This is something more than garden-variety procrastination. It's a deep-seated impatience with repetitive work that merely preserves a status quo rather than adding value. I'm not sure whether it's a character defect or a personality type, but I know I've got it—and that it would be a deadly liability in wooden boat stewardship.

I visited a friend who lives aboard a thirty-seven-foot sloop in a Seattle marina. "It's really no different than maintaining a house," he explained. "Except that if you put things off, your home sinks." Or as still another owner at the Lake Union show told me, "You've got to be very dedicated and very anal."

For a few days I actually considered Patty's startling proposition. Technically, it was feasible: we could convert our dry-land equity into this wooden boat and live aboard; the $400-a-month moorage fee would substitute for the interest we were paying on our mortgage. The sloop was breathtakingly beautiful. It promised a steep but exhilarating learning curve. It would rip us out of the ruts of predictable routine, and as the artist who scooped up the Chinese junk put it, sometimes in life we are well-advised to do crazy things. On the other hand: abandoning home and plunging life savings into a forty-five-foot sailboat when you don't know how to sail, don't even know whether you might *like* to sail, goes beyond crazy—it's reckless.

An embryo of an idea, not as precipitous but just as ridiculous and impulsive, stirred in my mind: I could build a sailboat.

Chapter 2

Why Build a Boat?

A PEASANT FISHERMAN IN Mexico or Malaysia has every reason in the world to build a boat, but a middle-class American in the suburbs may have to go to some trouble explaining and convincing.

If you live alone, no problem. You don't have to justify building a boat any more than you would making crab-and-gouda enchiladas for breakfast. No one needs to see you or be affected by either, and if you choose to report your adventure to friends, they can just write it off as one more charming eccentricity. Four years after that transfixing afternoon at the wooden boat show, however, Patty was dubious, and not without cause. Over the last several months I had been talking about building a sailboat with gradually increasing frequency, like a Geiger counter approaching a cache of plutonium. Every time I brought up my latest idea she would nod silently, her head bobbing in a small and noncommittal arc, neither asking questions nor supplying encouragement. I knew what this meant; no one married for thirty-five years remains oblivious to nonverbal communication.

I couldn't blame her. My history is littered with grand plans and colossal efforts that dribbled into inconsequential scrap heaps.

Through most of the 1970s I studied piano, first with Patty and then with a demanding concert pianist. I was a serious and dedicated student. I would come home from my job as a newspaper reporter around five most afternoons and hit the Yamaha grand for two hours of rigorous practice while Patty taught her young piano students in another room. I looked forward hungrily to that daily practice session because I loved the music I was playing, and because it provided mental release from the stresses of newspaper work.

Eventually, though, the piano imposed its own form of stress. I hit a plateau—it felt more like a concrete wall—where I couldn't seem to make any more progress. I'd made it into the minor leagues of the serious classical piano repertoire, playing the lesser Mozart and Beethoven sonatas, Chopin nocturnes and waltzes, and—a personal favorite—the Schubert C minor *Impromptu*. But I couldn't break through to the next level. I ached to play *big* Beethoven, like the fiendishly difficult *Waldstein* sonata. And I increasingly realized I wasn't going to get there, ever. I had enough musical ability to read a score and hear precisely the interpretation I wanted in my head, but I couldn't make my fingers realize it. I daydreamed about taking a year-long sabbatical and practicing *four* hours a day, the standard for concert pianists, but I knew even at that level of effort I would never be good enough to play anything like the *Waldstein* in public for paying customers. If I couldn't satisfy an imagined audience, it was equally unlikely that I could ever satisfy myself. And so I became a piano dropout at the age of thirty-five.

Periodically, the piano returns to haunt me, a nagging ghost of desire—and guilt. A few years ago Patty played the *Waldstein*, among other red-meat pieces by Bach, Brahms, and Brubeck, in a dedication recital for a new grand piano at her church. I assisted by turning pages and, when asked, coaching her practice sessions. This latter was a delicate balancing act, as anyone knows who's ever dared to critique a spouse's or lover's artistic work. The task became particularly tricky with the *Waldstein* because I was playing the son of a bitch, vicariously, through her. I wanted to take control, to make it *my* performance. But we both understood what was happening, she put up her usual stiff resistance to letting anyone push her around, and I throttled back on the suggestions that were arising essentially to satisfy *me*. And we stayed married.

Over dinner one evening, I tried to explain why I wanted—*needed*, even—to try building a boat.

I've been feeling more and more frustrated with my magazine work, I said. The assigned articles are getting shorter and shorter—most editors seem to think readers' attention spans expire in three minutes—and the pieces are predictable and flimsy. The work is just income—most of it doesn't *mean* anything to me.

"I know," she said.

"I've figured out a plan," I continued. "If I just discipline myself to work more efficiently, I can compress the same amount of shallow magazine reporting and writing into a shorter work day. I can finish by two or three in the afternoon and go out to the garage to work on the boat, and it'll be like a daily sabbatical. I need that different kind of fulfillment, creating something tangible with my hands, and something that isn't trivial."

She listened. She didn't counter, as many spouses might, that a sailboat *is* trivial. She understood that this would be something more than a grown-boy toy, and that what I was proposing was very different from going to a dealer and buying a factory-produced boat. I wanted to go deeper with her at this critical moment, to explain how I felt that building a boat could be an exercise in building character, but the concept was still too loosely formed in my mind to shape into words, even with my most intimate and trusted friend.

She decided to trust me, even with my checkered history of failed plans and imploded ambitions. "Well," she said, "you're not quite a boatbuilding virgin."

Four years earlier, acting on a weekend whim, we had taken the ferry over to Port Townsend, the fetching little Victorian seaport on the Olympic Peninsula that aspired in the 1880s to become the Boston of the Northwest. Planted conveniently where the Strait of Juan de Fuca turns the corner into Puget Sound, Port Townsend appeared to be the perfect port of call for sailing ships. Westerly winds in the strait would blow the vessels right to it, while if they had to continue up the calmer sound to Seattle or Tacoma it could add days to the sailors' voyages. Unfortunately, these ambitions were blossoming in the twilight of commercial sailing. The advent of steam-powered shipping scuttled Port Townsend's plans. A few generations later it would become the B&B capital of the Northwest, the one plausible modern use for all those overblown Victorian houses. The town also still harbors quite a few maritime cottage industries, one of which is a highly respected kit-kayak manufacturer, Pygmy Boats.

We hardly needed another kayak. We already had two factory-built fiberglass kayaks, and our only beef was that they were heavy lumps to heave onto our tall Subaru's roof rack. But to upgrade one's flotilla, any excuse will serve. A wood kayak could be substantially lighter—around thirty-five pounds instead of fifty-five—and much prettier as well. We walked into the Pygmy world headquarters and arranged to paddle several of their demo models around Point Hudson Harbor, conveniently right outside the shop. After an entertaining hour on the water, switching among five different boats, we bought the smallest model, the Arctic Tern 14. Its parts—precut pieces of ⅛-inch-thick marine plywood, a bolt of fiberglass cloth, and a few bits of hardware—all fit into a long, skinny box that might have been used to pack a tall floor lamp. I thought at the time, *Inside this scrawny box is a boat that's supposed to venture out on the Pacific Ocean!* It seemed no less preposterous than buying a forty-five-foot sloop that we wouldn't know how to sail: just cheaper.

When we got home I methodically swept the garage, cut open the box, and laid all the pieces out on the floor. It didn't look like a boat or a prayer of becoming one. I remembered a TV interview with Bill Clinton between his 1992 election and inauguration. "I feel a little like the dog that chased a pickup and actually caught it," he'd admitted. "Now what am I gonna do with it?" I felt like the dog-elect. I dug into my flimsy magazine assignments instead of the boat project, and didn't even touch the pile of plywood for the next three months.

What was going on? I wanted the kayak, and I wanted the challenge of building it. I had no rational reason to fear it—I had built a two-manual French baroque harpsichord from a kit in 1978, and it had turned out decently. The harpsichord's construction manual was a two-hundred-page book; the kayak's instructions barely ran forty pages. I fashioned a joke-excuse for my procrastination that seemed to have some plausible whiff of truth. "Nobody ever drowned because a harpsichord came apart in a concert." The real reason was darker than fear of trusting my life to inexpert craftsmanship. I was drinking at the time, but trying to closet it in a daily window of time that didn't compromise either my writing or my marriage. I feared that I couldn't squeeze both the drinking and boatbuilding into the same three- or four-hour weekday afternoon window.

After three months I ran dry of too-busy excuses and plunged into the project. Almost immediately I enjoyed a modest rush of success. Like most kit kayaks, Pygmy uses the stitch-and-glue method of construction, in which the builder "stitches" precut panels of the hull and deck together with wire, then solidifies the joints with thickened epoxy. It's a straightforward way to build a kayak, requiring no great skill. Occasionally a step in the instruction manual would be unclear, and somewhat to my own surprise, I felt no reluctance to call the Pygmy factory several times to ask for guidance. The employees I talked with were invariably helpful, clear, and they didn't charge anything for answering questions. The computer industry could learn something here, if it cared to.

The first serious test was fiberglassing the interior. To do this, you have to fit a rough-cut layer of fiberglass cloth fourteen feet long into the banana-shaped chamber of the hull, mix the liquid epoxy and hardener, ladle it evenly onto the glass to saturate the fibers, then squeegee away the excess, leaving no gaps, air pockets, or wrinkles; and complete the entire procedure in the thirty minutes before the epoxy begins to congeal. Panic is obviously not helpful. And panic, it seemed as I closed in on the last five minutes of the epoxy window, was the only rational response. The cloth wouldn't lie snug in some of the corners, and there was a panoply of wrinkles that seemed determined to survive. I'd had a drink to blunt the anxiety, and it wasn't working. Decision time: Jerk out the whole epoxy-saturated cloth, throw it away, clean out the hull, and try again the next afternoon—or let the blemishes stand and deal with them as well as possible later, with filler and sandpaper?

I let them stand.

Patty drove in from work a few minutes later. I was still tinkering with the cloth, delicately prodding it with brush and squeegee, trying to coax out the worst of its misbehavior. The wet epoxy was spectacularly glossy, and the mahogany of the hull was resplendent. Patty was enormously impressed.

"It's stunning," she said.

"Well, yes, but there are some problems."

For years she has been trying to retrain me to accept compliments without swatting at them, as if they were flies. She points out, correctly, that doing so deflates the person offering the compliment, that it insults her judgment. I've always felt that accepting an undeserved compliment is a moral lapse, like pocketing the benefit of a waiter's mistake on a restaurant check. I suspected this was going to be a recurring issue when I finished this kayak and began taking it out in public.

By this time I had completed enough steps successfully to convince myself that I could build the boat, but could I build it well? Could I lay the exterior fiberglass and epoxy smoothly, with no pimples or wrinkles? Could I make the hatches watertight? (Leaky hatches are the bane of countless kayaks, even many factory-built models.) Would the chine and sheer seams be strong enough to survive an unplanned beating? This last issue was, and is, critical: I wasn't planning to baby this boat by paddling only on calm lakes; the world—well, Puget Sound, at least—would be its oyster.

I have never been a notably sloppy craftsman, but neither am I meticulously good. If you were to size up a room I've painted, a bookcase I've refinished, or a car I've just washed, you would probably issue the same grades my high school teachers did: B average. Unrealized potential, could do better. Attitude problems. That "attitude" actually is a kind of value judgment, which I think is defensible in some circumstances. Let's say it takes an hour to do a Grade B car wash. Grade A would require another hour of detail work. Is the extra time worth it? For some people (and some cars), yes—and I wouldn't argue with anyone who consciously made that choice. To me, it isn't. I like my car, I don't love it. The B wash is enough to preserve the car's value and respectability. I'm constantly aware that time is a non-renewable resource, and I want to slot the extra hour it would take to make it an A somewhere else. I had the same attitude toward high school, although I couldn't have articulated it like this at the time. Back then, a mousy B average was enough to gain admission to most state universities. (Things have changed, not necessarily for the better.) That was my goal; I did just enough work to get there, and no more. There were too many other interesting things in high school that were begging for time. There still are.

The trouble with rationalizing mediocrity is that you can get used to it. The B average, or even the C, becomes the default mode. It feels so comfortable and normal that the effort to do A-level work on *anything* seems, by contrast, abnormal. Maybe *so* abnormal that it's impossible. We forget how to push ourselves to the highest level, how to muster all of our resources of imagination and concentration and patience to bear on a task. That's the tragedy of Willie Loman, aching to be recognized for greatness without ever *being* great. Which is "what most of us are doing, or dreaming about doing," as Arthur Miller later claimed in an interview. He might be right. Why else would *Death of a Salesman* resonate so deeply in our culture?

I dreamed of a Grade A slam dunk on the kayak, which deserved the effort. I also doubted I could pull it off. As the weeks passed, workmanship issues arose. Some of them were impediments of my own making. To keep some of the clutter off the deck, I decided to fit the hatches with a hidden system of bungee cords that would hold the lids down tight with tension from below. This simple concept proved phenomenally difficult in execution. I was no longer following instructions in the manual; I was creating something new. I carved a handful of L-shaped oak brackets to hook the bungees, but they had to be strengthened with sheaths of fiberglass and epoxy. That was a job for expert hands. I struggled for a week and inexpertly cobbled the system into existence. It worked adequately but looked awful—if you were to open a hatch and peer inside.

The boat's inside, in fact, was thoroughly blemished with pimpled and wrinkled fiberglass. Outside, from a dozen feet away, she looked spectacular. And once I got fully acquainted with her after a few sessions on Puget Sound, she performed spectacularly. Our two factory kayaks, both substantially larger and heavier, suddenly seemed about as responsive as bathtubs bobbing on the waves. The ultralight Pygmy accelerated faster, turned more crisply, and demanded more alertness if her occupant cared to stay upright in a churning sea. The hatches leaked only a little, and the hull seams showed no sign of distress when big waves lurched and kicked the little boat around. In a fond nod to her tiny dimensions, I named her *Plankton*.

Empowerment, inadequacy. I felt a considerable glow of accomplishment for building a boat that was not just seaworthy, but remarkably capable. But was that really such a big deal? Someone else had designed her, written the instruction manual, and precut all the critical pieces. All I had done was follow the instructions, imperfectly but not disastrously. I had assembled a kit, nothing more. The Pygmy catalog, in fact, goes out of its way to minimize the home builder's piddling contribution: "The building process takes no special skills. Hundreds of men and women with no prior woodworking experience build Pygmy boats each year." Apparently true. In the first year I paddled *Plankton* I saw dozens of Pygmys and other kit kayaks in the waters of Puget Sound, and most of them looked at least as good as mine. In the hidden recesses of the hull and under the hatches, I feared that they all looked better, and the few that I had a chance to inspect up close, in fact, did.

A year later I signed up for a ten-day course in kayak building at the Northwest School of Wooden Boatbuilding in Port Hadlock, another coastal town on the Olympic Peninsula fifty miles northwest of Seattle. This time it wasn't on a whim. The tuition was $850, and rental for a one-room cottage a few miles from the campus another $500. We would be learning how to build a wood-strip kayak, a quantum leap in complexity and beauty beyond the Pygmy kits. I had seen a couple of professional builder Joe Greenley's wood-strip kayaks, and they were floating sculptures. Greenley was the course's instructor.

My enduring memory from the first day of the course is: linguine. Immediately following introductions, we watched and sort of helped Greenley mill a stack of cedar planks into strips ¾ of an inch wide, ³⁄₁₆ of an inch thick, and 18 feet long. They seemed as limp as wet linguine and just about as elegant, and it was impossible to imagine how this nest of noodles was going to become a serious, seagoing boat.

Wood-strip construction is an ingenious but labor-intensive technique for building small boats. Its origins are murky, but it may have been devised by frugal Maine fishermen as a way of using the free offcuts tossed out by sawmills. To strip-plank a hull, you cut out plywood cross sections of the boat's shape at intervals of a foot and set them up along a spine called a "strongback." Then you bend the strips around the cross-section forms, glue them together, take out the forms, and sheathe the boat inside and out in fiberglass. Like an airplane fuselage, it's a lightweight, frameless structure in which the stressed skin provides all its strength. It's deceptively strong and rigid. I asked Greenley if such kayaks could take a beating in rocky surf landings. "That's not what most people use them for," he said. "But I could build an icebreaker this way if someone wanted it."

There were seven of us in the class, none with any real boat-building experience. Two were surgeons; I immediately assumed that their mental discipline and long practice in performing precision work with their hands would make them good boat-builders, then dismissed that as a cliché. The cliché proved to be true. There was a retired teacher, a retired electrical engineer, a retired airline pilot, a young guy trying to find himself, and me. Each of us, happily, seemed to have some skill that proved useful in the class. I was good at taking notes.

Greenley was good at building boats. And good at building, period. After just the first day, I was in awe of how efficiently and mindfully he worked. He never set a pencil or plane down and forgot where it was. He never seemed to become annoyed or frustrated by a mistake or difficulty; he would move from problem to solution in a straight line, without letting it get mired in any emotional muck in between. Do I need to say that Greenley's calm, rational, efficient manner of working contrasted starkly with mine? I suspected I might have something to learn here beyond how to make a boat out of cedar noodles.

He was no Zen philosopher, however. During a break I told him about my muddled work habits and asked how he'd managed to train himself to be so orderly and efficient. His answer was pure practicum: "Wear a canvas shop apron, and keep your most important tools in it—pencil, tape measure, knife, glue." He hadn't *had* to train his mind; the discipline was already there. He only had to buy an apron.

Greenley operated his business, Redfish Kayaks, as a one-man outfit. There wasn't enough profit margin to bring in employees, and anyway, I had trouble imagining anyone who could meet his standards of workmanship. He built six or seven kayaks a year, selling them for anywhere between $4,000 and $8,000 depending on the fanciness of the woodwork, and supplied "kits" consisting of milled cedar strips and plans. (Unlike Pygmy, he did not tell buyers they were easy.) He enjoyed talking about his customers; each boat had taken on an individual life because of them. One had staged a marriage proposal using his Redfish kayak: he took his girlfriend out paddling, and at an opportune moment staged a capsize in the Redfish. When his girlfriend, still upright in the other kayak, reached out to help him back into his boat, he tucked a ring into her hand. She accepted it. One "kit" builder reported to Greenley that the project had lifted him out of a profound depression. But another claimed that building a Redfish had precipitated his divorce.

"As far as I know, none of my kayaks has been involved in a conception or birth yet," Greenley told us.

Over the next nine days, we closed in on what began to look like a contradictory and self-defeating goal: we were building a boat of such breathtaking beauty that its eventual owner would surely be reluctant, even terrified, to put it in the water. Even in its raw form, festooned with staples and clamps and bits of masking tape and epoxy dribbles, the cedar radiated so much visual warmth it could have heated the boat shop through the coming winter. Why does anyone ever paint a wooden boat—or for that matter, a wooden house? The hull and deck, fitted together, had an organic sweep, like the sleek and graceful form of a dolphin: a curve ordained by nature. We students begin to openly covet her, masking our sin with humor. When we arrived at the shop one morning, Lynda, the retired teacher, discovered that a fly had gotten itself stuck overnight and died in the drying epoxy on the deck. "Don't worry," cooed Tom, one of the surgeons. "It's *my* boat."

One of us, in fact, would cart it home, for keeps. The plan was that in the final hour of class on the last day we would draw straws for it. The approaching lottery weighed increasingly on our minds, threatened to become an obsession. Greenley said he had made a mistake the last time he conducted the class, giving in when the students nagged him into holding the raffle early. "After that, the ones who didn't win all got a little sloppier with their work." I was torn between wanting *this boat*—it would save a bundle of time and money, and I knew I couldn't come nearly this close to perfection without Greenley hovering about—and building one that would be entirely my own. How many of us, out here in the twenty-first century, ever create something as beautiful and important as a boat, all by ourselves?

During another break, I asked Greenley how he'd feel if someone commissioned one of his kayaks to hang in a living room somewhere as a work of art—literally too beautiful to put in the water. It wasn't an academic question. A writer for *Town and Country* had just called to schedule an interview with Greenley, and in a kind of inverse snobbery, I told him that *Town and Country* subscribers are unlikely candidates for the hard work of sea kayaking. "I wouldn't mind," he said. "I take pride in my craftsmanship, whether it's functional or aesthetic." Greenley, I decided, was blessed not only with skilled hands but also with a mind that adamantly refused to overcomplicate things.

When the final Friday arrived, the class boat was about three-fourths completed. It lacked bulkheads, cockpit outfittings—seat and foot pegs—deck lines, a forward hatch, and final sanding and varnishing. Greenley set up the raffle with his characteristic precision: he disappeared into another room by himself and used a table saw to cut one of the cedar strip scraps into matchsticks, one of them exactly ¼ inch longer than the others. He returned, holding them in his fist, and we drew.

I won!

I spent a month doing the final finishing work in my garage—Greenley could have done it in two days, not counting the drying time for six coats of varnish—and christened her *Sea Major*. Since Patty's factory kayak was a less satisfying ride than mine, I gave her the new cedar-strip boat. *Sea Major* was a little high-strung in bumpy water, decidedly not a beginner's kayak, but as I had with *Plankton*, Patty found confidence in her once she had logged some paddling time. And I found I wasn't paranoid about either of us using her as an everyday kayak, picking up the inevitable dings and scratches from beach rocks and kayaker's clutter bungeed to the deck. I had made some mistakes in the final, unsupervised finishing work, and she wasn't too beautiful to put in the water.

Chapter 3

Looking for a Plan

Drinking and boatbuilding are two activities that should never, ever coincide, for an archipelago of obvious reasons. But they're not obvious to the determined drinker.

If I point a flashlight into *Plankton*'s hatches today, I can see several depressingly sloppy junctions where the bulkheads meet the interior sides of the hull and deck. Getting bulkheads to fit well is a difficult job under the best of circumstances, and I had figured to blunt the guilt-in-advance of not getting it right with a balm of vodka. Clefts of epoxy with the look and texture of dried oatmeal now form a memorial to Dr. Smirnoff. On the aft hatch cover, right out in the daylight, there's a wayward cut mark half an inch long where some fool saw veered away from the cutout line. It's filled with epoxy so it has no effect on the boat's structure or watertightness, but it's a permanent reminder of my condition on the afternoon I cut out the hatch. I've never told anyone what happened there, not even Patty, but I wouldn't have to. She knows.

I became an alcoholic unusually late in life, sometime in my late thirties. The date is vague because it was gradually and almost imperceptibly that I slipped over the line from normal drinking—an occasional cocktail after work, or a couple of glasses of wine with dinner—into drinking I *had* to do in order to face everyday life. Four or five years passed before I recognized that I had become an alcoholic, and then, surveying the options, I decided that instead of trying to get sober I would be a fully *functioning* alcoholic. And I was: in 1995, the last year we lived in Tucson, I wrote two books and a dozen magazine articles and taught two journalism courses at the university, all while sneaking about two-thirds of a bottle of cheap vodka every day. It felt like trying to hold together a house of cards in a blizzard. It was insanely difficult, physically and emotionally miserable, and finally doomed to fly apart.

Alcoholics who are fortunate enough to find a road to recovery will at some point look inward and try to discover *why* they drank, because that understanding appears to be an important piece of maintaining sobriety. It really isn't as complicated as most people imagine. We all drank because we had a disease, a chemical imbalance in the brain that caused us to crave alcohol beyond the point where a rational person would stop craving and drinking. Still, there is usually an emotional imbalance that parallels the chemical malfunction, and it's wise to try to deal with it.

Fear, more than anything, fueled my drinking. Until the past three years, there wasn't any time of my life that wasn't

bracketed in fear. Fear of failure, fear of criticism, fear of looking foolish, fear of punishment, fear of pain, fear of death,
fear of being found out. This last is a fascinating and pervasive
phobia that has only recently begun to get its due notice, and
that certainly has a high probability of surfacing whenever one
tries to build a boat. *Fear of being found out*—the hollow, gnawing
premonition that some morning the world will notice that you
don't really know enough to be doing what you're doing, that
you're an incompetent, a fraud, a poseur. Psychologists have
actually coined a term for it, "the imposter syndrome," and
have discovered that it haunts even some of the most obviously
successful people. I once plugged the phrase "felt I was a fraud"
into the Lexis-Nexis search engine and turned up hundreds
of hits—people who had used these exact words in published
autobiographies or interviews. Two names particularly jumped
out at me: Lena Horne and Mike Wallace.

I can't remember the exact point at which my youthful
arrogance—figuring I knew *everything*—tipped the other way
and I started to feel like I knew hardly anything, but it was
sometime in my mid- to late thirties. That's an interesting
coincidence with the onset of alcoholic drinking, if coincidence is what it was. All my life I've had a vast curiosity and
an enormous range of interests, but when this pivot occurred I
began to feel not at all like a polymath, but a dilettante. I had
skimmed a bit of superficial knowledge about a lot of things,
and was barely holding together this gridwork of pretenses.

There came one moment of relief when I learned I wasn't
alone. I was running a magazine at the time, a job that presented a dozen management problems every day that I wasn't

qualified to handle. Yet I was making the decisions—had to; the staff was too small to delegate. At the end of one particularly exhausting day I confided my feelings of ineptitude to a friend on the staff.

"That's exactly how I feel as a single mom," she said. "Every day I make decisions about a young human life that I'm not even remotely qualified to do. I keep thinking any day now, the Adult Police are going to come and take me away."

I began toying with recovery in 1996. I would take it seriously for weeks or months at a time, then treat myself to a relapse. I went to AA meetings regularly, occasionally even led them, but for years I couldn't fully accept the program. The concept of relying on a Higher Power seemed to be a permanent stumbling block. After years in the program I was more devoutly agnostic than ever; I found it impossible to believe in any kind of God that listened to human prayers and answered them—or not. What sense does a capricious God make, and what's the point of trusting it? The breakthrough came with a remarkably simple turnaround. I realized that Nature could serve perfectly well as my God if I accepted a baseline moral obligation to play a useful role in the network of life on earth—being an active steward of the environment and being useful to my fellow humans however possible. This meant staying fully conscious, not blurring my interaction with the world through the fog of alcohol. It may have been a philosophical contrivance, but what the hell: it worked.

I've brought up my history with alcohol because it's inextricably linked to the undertaking of building a boat. It's easy for a drinker to hatch a plan to build a sailboat—hell, let's make it a forty-foot schooner. Grandiose plans litter the dreamscapes of drunks. Actually doing it requires sobriety—not only for the physical coordination and judgment and sharp-tool handling, but also, at least in my case, for the courage to try it. I had to stop drinking to stop being paralyzed by the fear of failure.

When I began seriously contemplating a sailboat, I knew absolutely nothing about how to build one, but I had stumbled across a couple of inklings of how not to.

Not long before this, Patty and I had been driving up the east coast of Vancouver Island on one of my travel-story assignments. We stopped at the picturesque fishing village of Cowichan Bay and toured its Maritime Centre, which included a small wooden boat museum. There we studied a not-quite-finished twenty-seven-foot sloop parked at the wharf. A sign sparely outlined its history:

Started 1961. Worked on for 40 years. Given to Maritime Centre 2001.

Back in Seattle, I noticed this classified ad in the *Post-Intelligencer*:

50′ sailboat. You finish. $18,000 or best offer.

Pricing a bandsaw at my neighborhood Home Depot, I mentioned to the tool guy what I might be about to do with it. He laughed. "A man who used to work here is building a wooden sailboat, too. It's something like fifty-four feet. He admits he'll never finish it." I wasn't sure whether this was supposed to discourage me from buying a bandsaw, or make certain that I walked out with a lifetime supply of blades.

Among the seriously boatstricken there is an almost irresistible compulsion to launch an overly ambitious project, and among boats there is a secret pact to put down any stirrings of hubris in the community of Homo sapiens. Any half-built boat can find a way to outsmart its owner. The only defense is humility. Samual Devlin, a prolific boat designer and builder in Olympia, Washington, offers this caveat in the opening pages of his boatbuilding book:

> If this is your first boatbuilding project, it is wise to start with a small, simple boat. Building confidence and skill is more important than building the boat itself.

This wouldn't exactly be my first boatbuilding project, but it would be the first in which my own judgment and problem-solving creativity would enter into play. I had decided early on not to build a kit sailboat precisely because I knew I could succeed at it. I had built dozens of things from kits, from knockdown Danish teak furniture with those wordless cartoon "instructions" to that French baroque harpsichord. Building a kit tests your compliance and patience, but not much else. Even if you don't have much of either, and I don't, you can generally stumble through by testing the way things fit together until something clicks.

I wanted more of a character-building project, though not one that would last forty years. It seemed reasonable to try to find a plan for a boat that I could build in one year. Projects that have clearly visible goalposts are the most likely to get completed.

It also had to be small. Nobody works on a boat outdoors through a Seattle rainy season, which lasts nine months; and our typically suburban neighborhood association also has a rule against storing any boat outside. In an uncharacteristic experiment in thinking through a problem ahead of itself, I measured my garage, drew its plan to scale, and tried to project not only how a boat would take shape in the space, but also how I could move around to work on it. The largest boat that could comfortably be born in the space I had would be about fourteen feet long.

I felt a wave of disappointment. Could a fourteen-foot sailing dinghy function as a serious boat? Would it serve as a character builder, a challenging enough step beyond the kayak projects?

I made a run to the public library and trucked home a foot-high pile of books such as *Building Classic Small Craft* and *Boatbuilding for Beginners.* They were lavish with illustrated instructions, and most showed the tatters and smudges of volumes that have been checked out and pawed through by many prospective hands. Projecting from the condition of the books, you would expect to see swarms of small, amateur-built wooden boats plying Puget Sound and Lake Washington. You don't. Here is what happens: Fifty people check out this same pile of books. Forty-eight spend a couple of hours turning the pages, then say to themselves, "Sure looks like a lot of work. Say, I think I'll have a beer." The forty-ninth will actually embark on a project, and turn out either a nice little watercraft or, after forty years, a donation to a wooden boat museum. The fiftieth will go look for an easier way to build a boat, which is what I decided to do.

The books I'd checked out were mainly about traditional wooden boatbuilding, which is essentially traditional wooden *ship*building, just scaled down and made lighter. You build a framework of wooden ribs, usually oak, that looks remarkably like the skeleton of a large sea mammal, then bend a skin of wooden planks around it and caulk the seams between the planks. Wooden boats and ships have been built in exactly this way since the fifteenth century. (The earlier Viking shipwrights built the skin first, then inserted strengthening frame members into it—a much less robust form of construction. The invention of plank-on-frame construction made Columbus and Magellan possible, and then cannon-carrying warships.) I discovered compelling reasons to not want to build this kind of boat. The first was that it would involve making a fire-and-water contraption to steam the ribs, like giant Chinese dumplings, in order to bend them. This sounded terrifying from beginning to end. Another was that a plank-on-frame boat is notoriously impractical if you're planning to store it out of water, which I would have to. When it's afloat, the planks absorb water and expand to seal the seams, then naturally dry and shrink when the boat is taken out. The happy skipper can look forward to hours of bailing every time this cycle is repeated. Finally, I wanted a lightweight, beachable boat—something that wouldn't be a monumental struggle to schlep around on land, and rig and launch. One of the reasons there's always a lavish supply of used boats on the market is that their owners have realized, belatedly, that the work of boat ownership outweighs the fun.

Small and simple was obviously the most promising way to go.

Still, I almost got seduced by a thoroughly traditional day-sailer called the Haven 12½, designed by Joel White, son of the great E. B. White. No amateur boatbuilder is immune to romantic folly, and the genetic link between E. B. and the Haven formed a thoroughly irrational and compelling pull. I discovered the slim collection *Essays of E. B. White* in 1976, and it was the lighthouse that first began to draw me away from formulaic newspaper writing. White's graceful, evocative prose is a lot like sailing—it rarely takes the shortest line between two points, but the meandering tacks can be full of unexpected pleasures and insights. Joel White's design was a respectful update of the Herreshoff 12½, an exquisite classic sloop built in Nathanael Herreshoff's Rhode Island boat shop from 1914 to 1943. If there is a more heartbreakingly beautiful small boat in existence, there doesn't need to be. I spent several hours studying Joel White's meticulous instructions and decided, reluctantly, that the Haven 12½'s deceptive complexity would form a disastrous trap—at least for me. In an introduction that echoed the craftsmanship of his father's prose, Joel White warned:

> The construction methods and the fine detailing are so much
> an integral part of the boats that to build one in a slapdash
> and crude manner is a sure invitation to disappointment in the
> finished product.

I felt chastised, and I haven't even built one.

The wooden boat revival that began in the 1970s, fortunately, hasn't only been a resurgence of traditional practices. A number of builders have devised ways to use modern inventions, most notably fiberglass and epoxy—the latter scornfully termed "glop" by the hard-core traditionalists. When I stumbled onto Sam Devlin's online catalog, and then his book *Devlin's Boat Building: How to Build Any Boat the Stitch-and-Glue Way*, I felt like I'd found a friend and ally.

The "stitch-and-glue way" needs more elegant terminology— it sounds like scrap-pile boatbuilding. In fact, it's thoroughly elegant in the technological sense, having more in common with modern jetliner construction than with a traditional wooden boat. There is no rib cage; the stressed plywood skin of the boat, reinforced with bulkheads, provides all the rigidity the structure needs. The skin wears an invisible jacket of fiberglass and epoxy, which renders it perfectly waterproof and impervious to rot. It's lightweight, so the boat displaces less water and consequently sails faster in light wind. Its history is short but entangled, involving inventors on various continents who apparently weren't aware of what the others were doing. The first popular surge of stitch-and-glue homemade boats, however, was cooked up by the *London Daily Mirror* in 1962, which promoted BBC do-it-yourself expert Barry Bucknell's simple design for an eleven-foot sailing dinghy. The still-popular Mirror Dinghy made modern sailing accessible to the British working class.

Plankton was a stitch-and-glue kayak, so I had had a little experience with the procedure. It still isn't as easy as enthusiasts like Devlin love to claim. "It's no harder and no more complicated than building a garden shed," Devlin chirps in the opening chapter of his book. No, not if your taste in garden sheds includes walls with compound curves, a fiberglassed roof, and a sail rig. I knew from building *Plankton* and *Sea Major* how many things can go wrong, how a trickle of small, unnoticed errors can build into a flood of trouble, and how much I had left to learn about building any kind of boat.

Devlin's catalog of designs included a lovely little sloop called Nancy's China, whimsically named in the 1980s after the ritzy china that Nancy Reagan ordered for the White House in the depths of a recession. Devlin suggested that one of the boats could be built for about the same cost as one of Nancy's place settings. At just over fifteen feet, it was a slight overmatch for my space, but I figured I could squeeze myself around the ends to work on it (note here the early warning signs of ambition/hubris). Devlin even offered an ingenious new version that uses an auxiliary electric motor with two twelve-volt batteries and a solar-cell panel for recharging them underway. Nancy's China was a floating showcase of environmental virtue. I ordered study plans—an incomplete version of the full blueprints—for $15.

Doug Lee, one of the physicians in the oncology clinic where Patty works as a nurse, had recently bought a Nancy's China built in Devlin's own shop, so I made a Saturday afternoon appointment to look at her. "She's a salty little boat," Doug said. "She's very forgiving to sail." I crawled over, around, and through her for an hour, taking notes and pictures. Between the study plans and this in-the-flesh example, I cataloged about forty things I had no idea how to do. It looked nearly as intimidating as Joel White's Haven 12½.

Isn't there more significance in achieving a monumental, overwhelming goal than in accomplishing something that looks manageable from the outset? It's what our culture teaches us at every turn: Sinatra crooning "The Impossible Dream," Edmund Hillary crowing on return from Everest, "We knocked the bastard off!" A couple of decades ago a New York investment magazine publisher named Gilbert Kaplan immersed himself in Mahler's gargantuan *Resurrection* symphony, took conducting lessons, hired an orchestra, and knocked the bastard off—to critical acclaim, even—in Carnegie Hall. He didn't bother with training wheels, like maybe conducting a Rossini overture or two for practice. (I've long been in awe of Kaplan, especially since I've conducted the *Resurrection* myself—at home alone with a miniature score, a pencil baton, and the Chicago Symphony on the stereo.)

I chewed on the prospect of building a Nancy's China for several days and finally consulted Jeff Kissinger, a carpenter friend who races motorcycles and resembles Hercules. I expected him to pile on the encouragement, urge me to go for it. Instead, he offered a gentle helping of Zen.

"You need to think of this as a ladder of little steps, and conceive of each one as something joyful," he said. "When you're done, you don't want to look back on this and be reminded of how miserable you were at some parts of it. And if you feel burdened or resentful at any stage, you'll build that into the boat."

A possibly less burdening alternative was Devlin's Zephyr, a 13½-foot sailing dinghy based loosely on the little duck-hunting skiffs called "melonseeds" that were popular around the bays of southern New Jersey in the late 1800s. Devlin's brief catalog description called her "stable and remarkably fast . . . the type of boat that you can both teach your kids to sail with, and keep yourself satisfied on a spirited evening sail at the end of the day's struggles." A Zephyr, he claimed, could be built in a little over one hundred hours.

I ordered the complete plans for $65 and discovered a remarkably simple, elemental sailboat that had none of the complex features of Nancy's China—no cabin, no provision for a motor, no solar panel, a single sail instead of the mainsail and jib sloop rig. It wasn't at all homely, but it appeared to be . . . honestly, a bit rustic. I figured I could maybe build it in two hundred hours. For a person whose leading character defect is impatience, I am a remarkably slow learner. I had no illusions about being able to work efficiently or intuitively, and I was factoring in the certainty of making cascades of mistakes and doubling back to fix them.

Patty and I also suspected we needed a very small, lightweight, simple boat in which to learn sailing—something whose response to a stupid move with the sail or rudder will be to plop over and pitch the offending skipper into the water, rather than to plow out of control into a marina and t-bone a Microsoft millionaire's yacht. The Zephyr would be so modest, so unobtrusive, so slow—Devlin's "remarkably fast" in the universe of sailing actually means 4 or 5 knots—that it would be absolutely harmless. If the Haven 12½ is the distillation of pure beauty and Nancy's China an energy-conservation showpiece, the Zephyr could be just a quiet testament to the almost-forgotten virtues of simplicity and humility. It felt like a plan.

CHAPTER 4

IMPATIENCE

THERE ARE NOT MANY absolutes in the design and construction of boats, as you can readily see just from poking around Seattle's assorted waterfronts. There are boats that look like and function as houses, boats that amount to nautical motorcycles, and boats that drive up out of the water to become cars or buses. There are boats that resemble overgrown washtubs and boats that look like mahogany rockets. There are boats built out of every conceivable material, and at least one that is inconceivable: concrete. (When I first raided the library for boatbuilding books I passed up the *Manual of Ferro-Cement Boat Building*, not regretfully.) But one rule that nobody ever violates is that a boat must be absolutely symmetrical, at least wherever it meets the water. A warped boat is a lurid embarrassment to its builder and an insult to the forms in nature from which it derives both its beauty and functionality. Have you ever seen an asymmetrical porpoise? Could you respect a shark whose port side was taller than its starboard?

Even before I ordered a stick of wood, I worried about cutting out the Zephyr's hull pieces precisely and stitch-and-gluing them accurately. In his book, Sam Devlin himself admits he once had to abandon a half-built boat because he glued it up ¾ of an inch out of square. I realized I was going to have to teach myself a new way of working if I were to have any hope of doing it right: more patient, more careful, more focused. No, deeper than that: more *dedicated* to an ideal of quality.

Like a million or two others, I read Robert Pirsig's modern classic *Zen and the Art of Motorcycle Maintenance* in 1975 and struggled to digest his philosophical pursuit of the ghost of Quality—he capitalizes the word to place it on the same plane as the Buddha, a commodity both physical and spiritual. In the course of the book Pirsig throws off much wonderful, practical advice that can be helpful to a boatbuilder, as well as to a motorcycle mechanic or a mountain climber, such as to live fully in the moment of each step, keeping eyes *off* the prize. "To live only for some future goal is shallow. It's the sides of the mountain which sustain life, not the top." The more he chases the definition of Quality, though, the more tangled it becomes. Eventually I gave up trying to understand it, except for this simple and profound connection:

> I think it's important now to tie care to Quality by pointing out that care and Quality are internal and external aspects of the same thing. A person who sees Quality and feels it as he works is a person who cares. A person who cares about what

he sees and does is a person who's bound to have some characteristics of Quality.

Often, I think, quality eludes us because we're caring about the wrong things. More precisely, our *institutions* are caring about the wrong things. Quality is conspicuously absent in much of the vast buffet of consumer goods and services we encounter every day, which at first seems paradoxical because there are so many forces at work today that ought to be enhancing and insuring it. Thanks to the global marketplace, competition in every arena is fiercer than at any time in history. Designers and engineers are working seventy-hour weeks. Laser-wielding robots assemble products to infinitesimal tolerances. The reason all this still doesn't add up to quality is that so much of industry's effort is being diverted away from the actual service or thing that's being created, and instead working on all the peripheral aspects: value engineering, marketing, advertising, packaging, creating the illusion of advantage over the competition. Nobody markets a cell phone today claiming it's more reliable and more durable. The parameters are inevitably more style and more features. The thing will be obsolete in a couple of years anyway, so it's presumed the buyer doesn't care how well it's made. Actually, I do. I don't give a flip about the camera, the video game parlor, or the ringtone library in my phone; I just want it to not drop calls in midstream—in other words, to be a good phone. But that's not what phones today are about.

As an amateur boatbuilder, I figured my venture would be a little easier because I didn't need to care about anything but the end quality of the object itself. I wouldn't have to make it appeal to anyone outside my household, wouldn't need to advertise it, didn't care about the efficiency of my personal manufacturing process. It wouldn't matter whether I took five hours or fifty hours to cut out the pieces of the hull, it only mattered that I do it correctly. I recalled a bumper sticker I once saw that maybe encapsulated a deeper truth than its author intended:

AMATEURS BUILT THE ARK.

PROFESSIONALS BUILT THE TITANIC.

I wondered whether some of the attitude of amateur care I planned to lavish on my boat would automatically leak over into the other arenas of my life, or whether I would have to struggle to make a conscious transfer. And would a transfer even be possible? I'd been finding it increasingly difficult to care about the majority of magazine assignments that had been coming my way the last few years. Maybe the assignments themselves had been so dumbed down by value engineering and marketing considerations that quality (beyond the basic level of accurate information) didn't matter. How many American workers and engineers and teachers feel like they're caught in that trap?

Maybe we all need to build sailboats—as a personal antidote to the forces that keep demanding more speed, more efficiency, and less substance.

I decided to prepare for the Zephyr both logistically and mentally by cleaning and organizing the garage. I hadn't cleaned it in two or three years. I had *never* organized it. Tools were tossed haphazardly in drawers, bird nests of rope and electrical cords were heaped in a storage closet, shelves held a random assortment of prehistoric paints and long-expired chemicals. Environments influence the acts we perform in them, and this one could not possibly have had a positive effect on the boat that was about to be created in it—quite aside from the fifteen minutes I would squander every time I needed to find a screwdriver. True, I wasn't particularly concerned with time management. But I needed to keep frustration and impatience at bay, because these are qualities that I could build into the boat if they started roiling and seething with nowhere else to go.

Garages are an important and, I think, frequently overlooked component of American ingenuity, providing incubation for a dazzling variety of enterprises. Hewlett-Packard and Apple computers were born in garages, as well as a Texas man's wheeled, stainless steel, multiple-turkey deep fryer. As long as Americans keep building houses with garages, we've got at least one advantage in industrial and intellectual competitiveness. The flip side is that the American garage is also a symbol of decadence and stagnation, serving as a repository for all the stuff that the typical household doesn't know what to do with (and therefore by definition doesn't actually need). The stuff shifts and redistributes itself throughout the landscape, migrating from garage to garage via eBay and lawn sales, like coastal dunes being heaped and rearranged by the wind.

I spent an astonishing five days renovating the baby boat's prospective room, and in the end I drafted a friend with a pickup to dump the junk—we'd do the earth a greater favor by decommissioning a load at the landfill than by reconstituting it in someone else's garage. A week later I couldn't recall a single item that departed—that's how important it had been to keep the stuff around.

I needed to give *Plankton* a new storage berth to open up more room, so I spent another afternoon building a couple of overhead shelves near the ceiling and devised a primitive pulley arrangement to hoist her up. I had to build the shelves and pulley system wrong so I could see why it didn't work, then take it down and try to rebuild it correctly. Three times, in fact. This process left a dozen unused holes for screws and U-bolts in my clever kayak hoist. I could have filled them but it seemed like a waste of time; they were out of any line of sight. But the shaky execution of this setup made me question my aptitude for building even a simple boat from scratch. I have a nearly immaculate inability to conceive an idea for a mechanical device in my head, draw it on paper, and then build it. I have to first build it wrong so I can see *why* it's wrong, then try to make it right. I can't make the direct conceptual leap from two-dimensional representation to three-dimensional reality.

I thought, I've got to do better than this on the Zephyr. But is this skill learnable at my age, or at any age at all? Or is it like tone deafness, the inability some people have to sing "Happy Birthday" in tune with the rest of the crowd?

When the garage finally seemed neat and vacant enough to accommodate an all-consuming project, I cleared an entire afternoon for a tool-buying expedition. This felt like the point of no return—once I bought all this stuff, I would be committed to building an actual boat. If I didn't, the only possible use for the tools would be to attack the mountain of Mr. Fixit projects that had been awaiting me around the house, most of them for years. This alone would be a colossal incentive for actually following through with the boat.

I spent $925 on tools, supplies, and essential accessories such as safety glasses and a filtering respirator. The centerpiece was a $400 Chinese-made bandsaw, which was actually a bandsaw *kit* that took two full afternoons to assemble. I used this process as practice for working carefully, methodically, and mindfully. The instructions appeared at least to have been edited by a native English speaker—there wasn't the usual "Put now the under widget to the deep bracket against firmly." Just the standard annoyances with nomenclature, figuring out which piece was which. How is a regular person supposed to know what a "trunnion support" looks like? It would cost the manufacturer, what, another two bucks to identify each part with a stick-on label?

When I finally prepared to switch it on I was apprehensive— I'd never operated an industrial-strength tool bristling with carbon steel teeth, let alone *built* one. I put on my new safety glasses and backed three feet away so I could prod the "on" switch with a stick, just in case the machine decided to kick the ninety-three-inch blade into orbit around my head. But nothing dramatic happened. It ran smoothly, issuing a soft baritone thrum that sounded almost sweet. I penciled a few sweeping curves on some scrap plywood and practiced cutting out vaguely boat-shaped pieces. Bandsaws are excellent for cutting curved lines, which is why they're more useful than table saws in boatbuilding. After half an hour's practice I unilaterally awarded myself a B in bandsaw management. I had thought earlier it would be a good idea to spend a couple of days practicing different kinds of cuts, but I seemed to be getting the hang of it quickly. And I was impatient to start on the Zephyr itself.

On the morning of September 26, 2005, a monster semi sidled up to the curb in front of my house, and the driver, a man named Milo, ambled to the door to announce that he had my marine plywood outside. Milo struck me as a throwback—not only because of his immense, tapered Norse-god beard, but also because he'd already phoned three times that morning to update me on the progress of his other deliveries and estimated time of arrival. As we started unloading, he told me he'd left Edensaw Woods in Port Townsend at 2 a.m. for a swath of ten mainland deliveries. "If I'm lucky with traffic, I'll make the 2:30 ferry and get home around 4," he said. There was no trace of anxiety or resentment over a fourteen-hour workday. Instead, he was giving me the impression that my dinky $360 order of plywood was the single most important item on his agenda for the day.

"What are you building?"

"A little fourteen-foot daysailer."

"Terrific. Can I see the plans?"

I unfolded the plans. He studied them approvingly and assured me, "You'll have a lot of fun."

"Have you built a boat?"

"I've thought about it," he said. "I'm afraid it'd become an obsession and I'd miss my kids' soccer games."

Milo and I delicately leaned the seven sheets of African okoume plywood against an inside wall of the garage, then he wished me luck and lumbered away for his next delivery. I had the feeling I'd been given a gift, that Milo's unhurried, friendly demeanor had left a residue of serenity that could form a baseline for my work on the Zephyr. Why hadn't he seemed rushed? Five minutes wasted making casual conversation with me could translate into missing the ferry later in the day. But he wasn't focused on the ferry, several hours in the future—for whatever reason, it was somehow important to him to make that *present* moment, my plywood delivery, a pleasurable encounter for both of us.

I'm compulsively responsible, like Milo, almost neurotic about phoning ahead if traffic is going to make me five minutes late to an appointment, but I don't share his easygoing patience. I hate wasting time. I'm exasperated by pointless complexity, which is why I refuse to slog through the 128-page instruction book for my cell phone and learn how to store someone's number in it. The procedure should be obvious and intuitive—and since it isn't, I'll punish the fathead engineers who designed it by not reading their instructions. Friends have gently told me they discern a particle of self-defeating irony in this position.

I had thought that this sailboat, once built, might be the perfect teaching tool for one who recognizes a need for more patience and serenity in his life. It won't be hurried, even by favorable winds. A powerboat is about a destination; a sailboat is about the journey. If you're planing over wave tops at 40 knots, you can hardly be aware of anything but the sensations of speed and the commotion needed to produce it. You're not going to hear the rhythm of the water slapping a shoreline or notice a seal shadowing the boat: everything is focused on the machinery. I have no objection to people who choose to enjoy the water in motorized form (except when they're too loud or too close or scaring wildlife away), but I don't think it's any way to get in touch with the environment—or by extension, with yourself. A sailboat can never overpower nature, only make use of her. That's a valuable metaphor for many facets of human endeavor, most of all for cultivating patience. I had absorbed all this from my few times out on sailboats, but what I needed now was to move my acceptance of the ordained-by-nature pace of sailing into the hands-on process of building the boat.

You could, in theory, construct a stitch-and-glue boat out of fir plywood from the local lumberyard, the same stuff you'd use for the doghouse roof or a quickie bookcase. But it wouldn't be good quality. Fir tends to splinter when it's sawed, and structure-weakening air gaps hide in the inner plies. The high-quality okoume plywood Milo had just delivered was intended for hardworking marine use, and it also had a fine, satiny grain and a faintly pinkish color. I kept running my hands over it, savoring the feel on my fingertips, until I suddenly realized the ridiculousness of the moment—I was wasting time. I now had everything I needed in hand to *begin the boat*.

The first step in making a stitch-and-glue boat is a large and frightening one: draw its major pieces on the plywood. This means scaling them up from the plans, a process boatbuilders call lofting. This would be almost effortless if boat parts were just rectangles and parallelograms, but such parts would only form a clunky, slab-sided barge. The beauty of a sailboat is in the organic sweep of its sheer, the line where hull meets deck;

and in the forward-thrusting chin of the bow and rake of the stern. Straight lines and right angles will kill any boat, aesthetically. Imprecision in lofting will kill it functionally. I decided I would try for a standard of accuracy of $\frac{1}{32}$ of an inch, the smallest increment I could measure.

Boatbuilding is caked in hoary traditions, and I encountered one of them right away. To transfer the shapes drawn in Devlin's plans to the plywood, I had to interpret a constellation of dimensions expressed like this:

1-1-7

1-4-6

2-3-1+

This is boatbuilding shorthand for feet-inches-eighths. So the first number, 1-1-7, means 1 foot, 1 inch, and $\frac{7}{8}$. It gets worse. The second number, 1-4-6, translates to 1 foot, 4 inches, and $\frac{6}{8}$, or, distilling the fraction as we were taught in fifth grade, $\frac{3}{4}$. The third number, 2-3-1+, means 2 feet, 3 inches, and $\frac{1}{8}$ *plus* $\frac{1}{16}$, making the fraction $\frac{3}{16}$. Or, as I had to mentally translate from Devlin's plan to my tape measure:

2-3-1+ = $27\frac{3}{16}$ inches

An hour of this, and my patience was strained almost to the snapping point—literally on the first act of the first afternoon of building the boat. And it stretched way past an hour. After I laid out all the points on the plywood for drawing the first two pieces—the two side panels of the hull, 14 feet long and roughly the shape of giant sword fern leaves—I checked every point and found three or four of them off by a fraction of an inch. I replotted the offenders, checked them again, and finally drew the long, sweeping arcs with a pencil, connecting the dots. Then I checked everything a third time, found yet another mistake or two, and redrew the lines. The whole process consumed three hours—just for drawing two side panels of the boat.

The ancient convention of 2-3-1+ struck me as a ridiculous affectation, a medievalism, a rejection of modern logic as absurd as the Flat Earth Society. We might as well be specifying boat dimensions in cubits. If I were president, we'd go metric at midnight tonight and 2-3-1+ would become 69.1 centimeters. I called the Northwest School of Wooden Boatbuilding to find out if anyone knew why boatbuilders cling to such an antique convention. "Boatbuilders are pretty simple people," an instructor named Tim Lee told me. "This just makes it simple to add and subtract fractions. It's really easy once you get used to it." He didn't make it sound like a scolding, but there was an implicit rebuke in his answer: Give it time. Work with it. Try a little patience.

Over the next three afternoons I drew all the Zephyr's pieces on the plywood, again checking each dimension three times. It didn't seem to get any easier, and I still had to correct several mistakes each time I checked. At least I was correcting them with an *eraser* instead of throwing away great slabs of expensive okoume that I'd cut out wrong. I couldn't recall being as meticulous—patient—as this about anything, ever. It was an unfamiliar feeling, but it seemed to carry a modest tingle of virtue.

At the same time, my newfound meticulousness was far from perfect or comprehensive. At least once a day I wasted a good five minutes looking for my pencil. I'd recently written a magazine profile of David Burch, who's taught marine navigation to more than 20,000 students since founding his Starpath School of Navigation in Seattle nearly thirty years ago. The best navigators, he told me, "are the ones who always set their pencils down in the same place every time." That echoed Joe Greenley's system of organizing his tools in a shop apron. What I wasn't getting from these guys was how one renovates a mind that's long been satisfied with a high ambient level of disorder.

When Patty came home from work on the third evening of lofting I proudly showed her our boat—in two-dimensional form, at least, penciled on plywood. I fumed again about the 2-3-1+ nonsense and about how many mistakes the unfamiliar notation had caused. She peered at the plans.

"Why didn't you just translate them into conventional measurements and write them on the plans?"

There was no possible reply—aside from grabbing a hammer and administering a dozen dope-whacks to my own skull. Later, as I pondered why I hadn't thought of Patty's obvious trouble-saver myself, I realized that grievances work like dams in the mind, frequently blocking the channels of constructive action. The dams acquire lives of their own, and it becomes more important to preserve that architecture than to open a way around them. I had *liked* bitching about the boatbuilding notation; it was an extension of my long-running exasperation with America's refusal to join the modern world in the metric system. But it wasn't a *logical* extension, because it had cost me time, trouble, and emotional energy. Patty's simple idea would have crumbled the dam, eliminated it as an issue.

I began cutting out boat parts the next day. Since the hull pieces were too big to feed into the bandsaw—which would have been the most accurate way to cut them—I used my handheld jigsaw and cut slightly wide of the lines I'd drawn, in effect making a slightly sloppy cut that I could then shave and refine with a block plane and coarse sandpaper. It sounds like a slow, clumsy, and imprecise process, and I'm sure there are German craftsmen who can cut such pieces with startling precision using the jigsaw alone. But I had to proceed by trial and error, and this way, at least, the errors remained small and manageable.

In a week of boatbuilding afternoons, I cut out all four pieces of the hull, the transom, and three bulkheads. I shaved the edges exactly to the pencil lines. I planed a forty-five-degree bevel on the inside edges of the hull bottom, where the two pieces were to meet in a V. All the pieces looked good, but I couldn't shake the ominous feeling that I'd made some kind of monumental mistake that wouldn't reveal itself until I put the boat together, when some critical part would turn up an inch too short. Remember the $125-million NASA Mars orbiter that burned up because rocket scientists confused their English and metric measurements? Something like that.

I worried that I might be edging into obsession, but I went back to the plans and measured all the pieces again—the fourth time, in all. I compared the angles on the bulkhead corners to the scale drawings on the plans. Every dimension of every piece appeared to be within $\frac{1}{16}$ of an inch of what Devlin had ordained. This was twice the tolerance for error I had firmly vowed to observe a week earlier, and I wondered if I might be doubling toward disaster. But the pieces were cut out, and they were the best I could do.

CHAPTER 5

IMPERFECTION

EVER SINCE I TURNED fifty a few years back, I've felt an insistent urge to try things I didn't know how to do, mostly things that have scared me stupid. In 2003 I spent a month hiking several big chunks of the Arizona Trail, just a few weeks after buying my first backpack. The trail winds eight hundred miles from Utah to Mexico, plunging into every damn canyon and over every freaking mountain the trail planners could find, nearly all of it serious wilderness. The next year a travel magazine asked me, a certifiable acrophobe, to take a one-day canyoneering course in Utah and write about it. I don't know why I agreed, but I did. The first rappel was twenty-five feet down into a frigid, bottomless pool in a vertical-walled slot canyon. The second, equally vertical, dropped forty feet. The third plunged 105 feet—a terrifying specification that our instructor, Nick

Wilkes, somehow had neglected to mention before we started out that morning.

There is something fundamentally, terribly wrong with the very idea of a human being voluntarily walking backward off a hundred-foot cliff and dangling from a scrawny rope over the stony jaws of eternity. I did it, but only because completing the two previous rappels had made it impossible to return to the starting point. On this third rappel my rope widget jammed halfway down and it took five agonizing minutes to weasel the last fifty feet. I interviewed Wilkes in the van on the way back. He said he'd shepherded students from four to eighty-five years old through his course. Some, he said, would avidly rent gear and tackle a nearby canyon on their own the next day; some would never attempt canyoneering again. I was reasonably certain I would be among the latter. Wilkes said, "But you know what? I've never had anyone finish the day feeling *less* self-esteem." He was at least right about that.

A month after starting work on the Zephyr, I was about to paddle 130 miles of the Columbia River in a kayak. Research had suggested that October, the least windy month, would be the best slot for the expedition. Summer's notorious winds hadn't sounded encouraging. When Pacific westerlies funnel into the Columbia Gorge, they collide with the downstream current flow to kick up steep, unpredictable waves. The October trip would interrupt work on the boat, it would undoubtedly rain on us, and mid-autumn dark would come early, but these seemed like the least of the Columbia's quiver of evils.

I was afraid of the river. I knew too little about its currents, weather patterns, and geography. I'd read stories about kayakers blithely paddling along when a monster container ship would silently materialize behind them, its approach masked by fog or riparian traffic noise. Commercial skippers refer to kayakers as "speed bumps." I was particularly concerned about the last twenty miles, where the river yawns into a four-mile-wide estuary that amplifies whatever meteorological mayhem the Pacific brews up. Overall, I was simply worried about the gross mismatch between the river's physical power and me—a channel of inexorably moving water, a quarter- to a half-mile across, versus a man in a fifty-five-pound fiberglass banana. (I would be taking my factory-built expedition kayak; *Plankton* and *Sea Major* are too small to carry a week's camping provisions.)

Some time back I pawed through Gail Sheehy's *New Passages* in search of something that could explain these midlife urges to push the envelope. My parents didn't suddenly turn adventurous in their forties or fifties, nor did any of their contemporaries that I knew of. If they felt restless and unfulfilled—and who doesn't, at times?—they didn't talk about it or do anything radical to try to fix it. Sheehy writes darkly about "the dissonance between the real self and the made-to-order self that the world has endorsed." I had come to believe that accepting that dissonance as a natural condition of life, not trying things because of fear of failure or disapproval, is a self-imposed prison. Trying, in contrast, gives us heart. A life vividly lived is its own reward.

I also think that not believing in the God, heaven, or hell of my parents' faith has, ironically, brewed up some late-coming courage. If one doesn't look forward to a purported life in paradise, then there's a powerful incentive to make the most of this one. At the same time, though, as I contemplated being kicked around on that almighty river, I thought: might be a lot less scary out there if I had a trusty angel to watch my ass.

My only companion on the Columbia would be an adventurous friend, Howard Greene, whom I'd met several years earlier on a kayak expedition on Lake Powell in Arizona and Utah. If you could fabricate the ideal hiking/kayaking/sailing buddy out of spare molecules, Howard is exactly what you'd come up with: knows what he's doing outdoors but doesn't hot-dog it, has a wide range of interests with which to fashion good conversation, and—best of all—seems utterly imperturbable out there. The previous year we had paddled up Puget Sound from Olympia to Seattle, a five-day, sixty-five-mile trip. On the fourth day I concocted a one-hundred-yard portage across an isthmus connecting two islands, neglecting to consider the tide. We arrived at low tide. The portage had sprawled to a quarter-mile. We unpacked our kayaks and under a blazing August afternoon sun undertook four round trips to schlep all our gear and boats across mud flats that felt like walking across brown yogurt. Howard never once muttered, "Moron!"

On the morning we drove down to our Columbia launch site we talked through the conditions we could encounter on the river—headwinds, wind waves, rain, fog, shipping traffic. A helpful Washington State Parks ranger had even informed us that bears swim out to the islands where we planned to camp. "My philosophy is to expect the worst," I said, "because then I'll be pleasantly surprised if it doesn't happen."

"I have that tendency, too," Howard admitted. "But what I try to do is avoid both optimism and pessimism—just deal with what comes."

We launched into the river at Beacon Rock, just downstream from the Columbia's westernmost dam and about 130 miles from the Pacific, and immediately slammed into a 20-knot headwind left over from summer. It kicked up chop big enough to slap our faces and bitterly resisted forward progress. Since it was early October with no melting snow in the Columbia's mountain watershed, the downstream current was sluggish. We vectored into the middle of the channel in search of stronger current to help push us along, but all we found was steeper waves. We groaned past anchored fishing boats, whose occupants stared as if they were watching a pair of Sasquatches bobbing by in bathtubs. There were no other kayaks. In seven days on the river we would see no other kayaks or canoes. There must have been a reason.

We earned just six miles in three hours and landed on a little alder-forested island at dusk to camp for the night. The wind died, the rain started. As ridiculous as it sounds now, I felt as though I should apologize to Howard—I'd worked out the schedule, so the lousy weather was clearly my fault. Just then occurred one of those small miracles of nature that makes it nearly impossible for a bystanding human to wallow in his own self-absorption. A black boomerang of Canada geese swept out of the sky and carved a turn low over the river, its outline soft and fuzzed in the fading gray light and drizzle. The geometric swirl of life was uniquely beautiful *because* of the lousy weather. I suddenly felt very glad we were there, and no longer afraid.

Over most of the next six days the Columbia behaved reasonably. It delivered a moving feast of scenery that passing motorists and boaters in faster watercraft never see, including several unadvertised waterfalls and, one morning when we launched at dawn, a kaleidoscope show of pink and orange fingers of light perforating the clouds. Another morning as we were gliding downriver in light fog, the water ahead appeared to elide seamlessly into cloud and sky, and we had the giddy sensation of paddling into infinity. The occasional big ship traffic proved to be no problem because the shipping channel was clearly marked on our chart and we simply stayed away from it.

The serious challenge was trying to figure out what the current was planning to do. Downstream from Portland the Columbia acquires a tidal flow as the Pacific tries to pour itself back into the river, and for a few hours twice each day the current chugs backward. It's no fun paddling against it, so each evening I struggled to chart the next day's itinerary so we would be off the water during peak hours of the reversed current. It proved agonizing to calculate. The farther downriver we moved, the earlier arrived the high tide, and the longer the ebb flow continued after the low tide. Informed guesswork was the best I could manage. Sometimes it didn't seem informed. On day five we struggled a long thirty miles to keep to the itinerary, and at least five of them were opposing the current. That night in my tent I read an essay by Ian Frazier and encountered a piercing truism that played directly on our expedition: "Among the cruelest tricks life plays is the way it puts the complicated part at the end, when the brain is declining into simplicity, and the simple part at the beginning, when the brain is fresh and has memory power to spare."

On the last day we were off before dawn—the current was going to slam us sometime late in the morning, and we had twenty-three miles to go to Astoria. It was eerily calm, no fog, and in half an hour the first light began to reveal exquisite patterns in the clouds—cats' pawprints stained red against the awakening sky. Something about that formation stirred a vaguely uneasy memory, but I didn't turn on the marine radio I kept in my life jacket. I had checked the forecast at ten the night before, and it was nothing unusual—light rain, moderate wind.

We paddled hard for three hours, the current turned, and there wasn't anyplace to take refuge except the uninviting sloughs that rake some mucky islands. We kept going. The midday sky darkened and then began to droop like an army tarp. Shifting winds clawed at us from assorted directions, as if probing for vulnerability. Astoria was six miles away, but conditions were looking increasingly ominous, and we saw on the chart that we had a bail-out option—a navigable creek that led to a county park. We ran for it.

The rain slammed in just after we dragged the kayaks onto the grass. I switched on my cell phone and picked up three overnight messages from Patty back in Seattle, each with an increasingly anxious edge to her voice. The forecast had changed radically through the night; Astoria weather now called for 30- to 40-knot winds and heavy rain. They meant it. By the time we caught a ride into town, the Columbia was olive green and whipped with foam. The vast estuary was sloshing like the bowl of a four-mile-wide Maytag.

"We just dodged a pretty big bullet," Howard said.

We had indeed. I thought back to a trio of duck hunters we'd encountered earlier at a riverbank shack. They were prepping for the season, outfitting their seventy-five-horsepower aluminum skiff with shotguns, ammunition, and a week's stash of beer. They had peppered us with questions: "Whadd'ya do if those things turn over—swim for shore?" They seemed befuddled why anyone would *want* to navigate the Columbia in an engineless boat. "Doesn't sound like fun to me," one said.

I told him I'd had moments of doubt myself. And in truth, all the usual reasons one might offer for undertaking such a trip ring flimsy when applied to this one. It wasn't a pioneering adventure; Lewis and Clark paddled much more river under vastly more challenging conditions (no maps, Gore-Tex jackets, or paddle-up dockside cafés). It wasn't a great endurance test; any reasonably fit kayaker could have done it. And to my great relief, it turned out to be much more about prudent judgment than courage. Maybe there *is* an angel of weenies, and she had diligently followed me from the Arizona Trail to the Columbia.

The real reasons for the trip may sound a little self-conscious and contrived when spelled out on paper, but out there on the river they *felt* wholly real and vital. One was to understand more about humanity's proper place in nature. The Columbia is an excellent venue to do this, because it's a river managed by human engineers while also a very complicated natural ecosystem; and a kayak is the perfect vehicle, because it's slow and quiet enough to permit contemplation and small enough that it had better make its way with respect and humility—qualities we humans can always use more of. The other reason was to redirect the interior current, the voice inside the head that admonishes: *keep your eye on the ball, don't get distracted, avoid forays into things that may not work out.* The river metaphorically suggests another way to live, one that applies to an expedition of no great consequence, or to the building of a sailboat. The river meanders, backs up, forms islands that are of no immediate use for anything. But it keeps moving, forming an essential part of the grand circulatory system of nature. We can do worse than live like that.

No elves visited the garage during my week on the Columbia to assemble the Zephyr's hull pieces. They all lay where I left them, propped flat against the garage wall, fuzzed with a dull fog of sawdust. They looked about as substantial as cardboard cutouts awaiting assembly for a Sunday school skit about Noah and the Flood.

But the pieces were ready to assume a three-dimensional shape, to start becoming my nine-cubit ark. All I needed was a roll of baling wire.

This is the "stitch" part of stitch-and-glue boatbuilding. It works like this: You lay the two matching pieces of the hull bottom together, drill a series of small holes six inches apart through both pieces near the edges where they are to join, slip a short piece of baling wire through each pair of holes, then twist the ends together. After all these sutures are in, you can spread open the two hull panels like a book and tighten the wires to close the joint snugly. Then you wire the side panels to the bottom in the same way. The wires function like clamps to hold the hull pieces in position for gluing; they'll later be taken out and the holes filled.

I made a quick run to Home Depot for baling wire. There wasn't any on the rope aisle nor the "fastener" aisle. None in the electrical department where they stocked other kinds of wire. When I finally tracked down an attendant, he looked as baffled as if I'd asked for moon rocks. He'd never heard of baling wire, and he said the store didn't carry anything like what I was describing.

A three-acre hardware store doesn't have *baling wire?* My first reaction was that it's another marker of our disposable-everything ethic in which the creative fixing of things is a vanished skill. On reflection, that's not really the case. Household creativity hasn't evaporated; its texture has changed. Today's fixit project is more likely to be finding a way to make a snotty computer do something it doesn't feel like doing.

I finally located a five-hundred-foot roll of baling wire at a farm supply store, the last of its kind in our no-longer-rural suburb, and I was ready to sew.

Wiring the hull together was a two-hour job that took me six hours over two afternoons. I put in several dozen of the stitches the wrong way, and it became apparent that if I persisted in tightening them to make the two hull bottom halves pull together, that I was going to break something—most notably the two halves. I reread a page of Devlin's book more carefully and discovered the warning was there all the time. I'd skipped over it. It's an old habit, closely related to never, ever wanting to be told how to do something—a problem with authority even in a benign, helpful form. It was going to cause trouble on this boat if I didn't start paying more attention.

Finally the pieces all fit together and almost magically there sprang into being the basic form of a boat: two bottom halves, two side panels, and the transom. In the evening I sneaked out to the garage several times and just stood there rubbing my eyes over it, feeling thoroughly awed—not at the fruit of my shaky craftsmanship but at the emergence of such an essentially beautiful organic shape from a nondescript stack of wood. In detail, of course, the boat-to-be looked awful. The twisted wires poking out every six inches were as elegant as a barbed-wire fence, and there were a couple of ominous air gaps where the transom (almost) met the hull sides and where the pointy ends of the bow (didn't quite) come together. No casual passerby who sees a stitch-and-glue boat at this stage of construction is likely to want to go for a sail when it's finished. Like sausage, you don't want to visit it in the formative stages.

I commandeered a portable steam gadget we bought for cleaning kitchen grease off appliances and over the next four days periodically huffed steam at the extreme bend of the side panels near the bow. When the wood was hot and saturated, I would quickly pull out half a dozen stitches and slip new ones in, tightening them up. The ¼-inch gap closed by another ¹⁄₁₆ of an inch each day, and finally the panels kissed at the bow. I had no idea whether this was a constitutional plywood-torture technique, but it seemed to have worked.

The daylight seeping through the other end of the boat, however, couldn't be dealt with in the same way. The transom—the flat panel that keeps the pesky sea out of the back of the boat—just didn't fit. There was a slim triangular gap on one side that widened to ³⁄₁₆ of an inch at its worst end. I didn't get it—if every dimension of every piece was accurate to a tolerance of $\frac{1}{16}$, what was causing the problem? And should I be worried? (I was.) I considered cutting a shim of scrap plywood to wedge into the gap, which would be structurally sound and invisible once it was epoxied and painted, but that seemed somehow like cheating—a kind of corruption of the soul of the boat, if not its functionality or surface beauty. I made a cardboard template and sawed out a new transom, which meant that in a month or two I would have to buy another $81 sheet of okoume plywood. This solution made no rational sense, it just *felt* like the right thing to do. I was identifying with this boat just as Steinbeck had predicted, building a "man-shaped soul" into it. That soul would not be perfect, but it had to contain some integrity.

I wedged the three bulkheads into the hull, temporarily tacking them in place with small nails. More air gaps appeared. The bulkheads stuck up as much as $\frac{1}{4}$ inch over the sides of the hull, which they weren't supposed to. The fractions-of-an-inch discrepancies seemed to be growing and multiplying like malignant tumors. I made a giant duct-tape bandage to try to pull the hull closer to its prescribed form. It all seemed ominously sloppy, even though it was actually in better shape than when I first gazed rapturously at the newly formed hull a few days back. Patty didn't seem to understand my worries. She took photos of the hull and e-mailed them to her brother in Dallas, who's an industrial engineer and a skilled weekend craftsman. He wrote back:

> Wow, Larry, your boat is looking great. I seem to remember you said this was not a kit—so you cut all those great curves.

The baling wire and duct tape are touching. It's nice to know that deep down inside you're still a Texan.

Love, Chris

We've had a decades-long, mostly good-natured battle over our mutual Texas roots, which I ran away from and he still embraces. His jab set me thinking, though, about the improvisatory spirit of the frontier—and vestiges of it do still exist in Texas—as opposed to the obsessive perfectionism that I felt in danger of becoming stuck in. It seemed worth pulling back for some perspective. Is there a level of imperfection in a project like this that's actually healthy and wise? If so, how do you determine where it is?

One of the boatbuilding books I read at the outset argued, sensibly enough, for balance. "Don't look for perfection," advised Greg Rössel in *Building Small Boats*. "We're not building a Steinway piano. The goal is just good old-fashioned clean workmanship—a job that fits well and looks good." The perfectionist's automatically obsessive mind, though, will take these very words and grow all kinds of justifications for monomaniacal attention to detail. "'Good old-fashioned clean workmanship' *is* perfection," he'll argue. "Why shouldn't a boat have the same level of craftsmanship as a Steinway—or even better? Nobody's life depends on a piano."

The trouble with perfectionism, of course, is that the road to paralysis is paved with it. I've seen it among my university writing students, who can't meet class deadlines because they're afraid their work won't cut it—even though the continuing education courses I now teach are nongraded. It's the underlying cause of most outbreaks of writer's block among students and professionals alike. I don't know how much it helps, but at some point in every course I pass out a micro-essay I wrote on the syndrome. Here's part of it:

The Perfect Writer

> Perfectionists are unhappy writers, and sometimes surprisingly lousy ones as well. So make yourself into a precisionist instead. Strive to be precise in your descriptions of things. Be scrupulously accurate; check everything before letting a manuscript out of your hands. Review every sentence to make sure that it's clear, grammatically clean, and says precisely and directly what you want it to say. Omit unnecessary words. But after you've done all this, don't kick yourself if you feel you haven't lit up the night with your writing. Accept craft as being just as worthy as art. Just telling a story clearly is a wonderful accomplishment. . . .

I'm fairly good at taking my own prescription when I'm writing, because I used to suffer miserably over trying to render it perfect, and don't care to revive the experience. But I was naturally less confident at boatbuilding and unsure how strictly to apply the principle of precision. If my $\frac{1}{32}$-of-an-inch standard was unrealistic—and I was now convinced it had been—what *is* both adequate and attainable? Does the builder actually fail a moral obligation to the integrity of the design and materials if he simply covers up a mistake, like using a shim to plug a gap between bulkhead and hull?

A British industrial designer and art professor named David Pye confronted these issues and more in a now-classic book published nearly forty years ago, *The Nature and Art of Workmanship*.

Pye laid out a distinction between what he called the "work-manship of risk" and the "workmanship of certainty." The first involves the creation of a unique object by hand, something that reflects its maker's judgment and skill and cannot be made in exactly the same way twice—thus the "risk." The latter is precision mass production, the results guaranteed to conform to the designer's intention every time. Pye was not damning a world increasingly pervaded by the workmanship of certainty. (Imagine, for example, if books were still copied out by scribes instead of printed—how many of us would even bother with literacy?) But he believed that keeping high-quality workman-ship of risk alive was so important that it went right to the heart of civilization itself: "To do a thing in style is to set oneself standards of behaviour in the belief that the manner of doing anything has a certain aesthetic importance of its own independent of what is done. This belief is the basis of ordinary decent behaviour according to the customs of any society." Pye seemed to be saying that if I covered up sloppy workmanship, it was not merely a disservice to Devlin, but a moral cave-in that threatened the foundations of civilization. It isn't that the world would be poorer if deprived of one exem-plary wooden boat, but that compromised standards inexorably creep from one arena of one's life to others, and the decay then ripples outward to infest society as a whole. It's a relative of Rudy Giuliani's conviction that cleaning up graffiti improves law and order generally. Giuliani put it succinctly in a 1997 may-oral speech: "Graffiti creates an impression of disorder and of lawlessness. A city tainted by vandalism invites more vandalism and more serious crime because it sends the message that the city doesn't care and isn't paying attention."

Wouldn't "decent behaviour," conversely, also have a ripple effect that reverberates from one side of the pond of human conduct to the other? For example, if you go to work in a place where the corporate culture is one of respect for other workers, wouldn't that culture translate into respect for customers and for the work itself? All this was forming a nagging counter to my long-practiced belief that *some* things don't need to be done particularly well.

I pondered these questions for a couple of days while I also considered my growing gaps and bulkhead stick-ups. I was on the brink of boatbuilder's block. Patty said I should call Devlin and ask his advice. It was an eminently sensible suggestion that I didn't take because I was afraid he'd tell me to throw the pieces away and start over. Finally, the threat of having to ask for help opened up the blockage. I decided that ego could be used as a litmus to test whether a particular piece or joint on the boat is good enough.

Here's how it would work. The first question would be: Is it functionally good and safe, as far as anyone can know? If not, something clearly has to be rebuilt. If it is, then comes the second question: Does it need to look better so that other people will think well of the builder? In other words, is ego-fulfillment the prime motivation? If so, the extra work wouldn't really be essential.

This referred back to the concept of "deep beauty," as I defined it early on. Deep beauty respects materials, function, and the user's needs. If a person actually *needs* a boat that generates waves of compliments everywhere it goes, then I supposed it would be legitimate to build it with immaculate detailing so as to accomplish exactly that. But I also suspected that person would not be a lot of fun to hang around with.

I asked Patty to come out to the garage and hold one end of my tape measure at the bow. I ran the other end to each corner of each bulkhead and the transom. Every dimension on the left (port) side matched every one on the right (starboard) within ⅛ of an inch. All the vertical dimensions lined up as well. My 13½-foot boat was within ⅛ inch of being perfectly symmetrical.

It seemed perfectly good enough.

CHAPTER 6

GLOP

IN THE SPRING OF 1839, Henry David Thoreau and his brother John built a wooden dory about the size of my Zephyr for a summer trip down the Concord and Merrimack rivers. The boat's construction "cost us a week's labor in the spring," Thoreau reported, and admitted it was no great triumph of craftsmanship. "It was strongly built but heavy, and hardly of better model than usual . . . [but it] proved a sufficient buoy for our purposes."

In the 492 pages of *A Week on the Concord and Merrimack Rivers*, the thrifty Thoreau spends just one paragraph describing his boat. Even though it was a recreational craft rather than a work-boat, he saw it as strictly utilitarian, not something in which he cared to invest a lot of labor or emotion. If something like it were to show up at a wooden boat festival today, everyone would scorn it: "Now there's a boat you should only row in the dark."

As our society has become increasingly affluent, we've become increasingly self-conscious about design, craftsmanship, and especially cachet among the things we own and do. Utilitarian is out, unless you dress it so elegantly that all actual utility is erased—like my neighborhood's $50,000 SUVs that their owners wouldn't dream of slogging through mud to deliver hikers to a remote trailhead.

The American twentieth century saw countless commodities and activities ascend to the level of connoisseurship, most filtering their way from the rich down to what used to be called the middle class. In *Bobos in Paradise*, David Brooks pegs it as "a cultural consequence of the information age." Newspapers, magazines, catalogs, television, and finally the Internet showed us what we needed to do and own in order to live tastefully. Modern Americans, for example, cultivate the art of coffee brewing and drinking (and spend for it) at a level that a generation ago would have astonished the average French citizen, who, after all, was drinking pretty decent coffee already. If a neighbor offers you coffee and then reaches into the pantry for a steel can of Maxwell House, you—and I—pass silent judgment: *way* uncool. Hikers in the mountains around Seattle self-consciously compare their gear—the carbide-tipped, shock absorber-equipped trekking poles, the altimeter/barometer/pulse monitor/wristwatches—at least as much as they talk scenery. (Hey, nature will be around forever. The trekking poles will be obsolete by next summer.)

By nature and purpose, a little daysailer ought to be simple and utilitarian. Historically, they all were. The first Star-class sloops, which appeared in New York in 1911 and sparked the revolutionary idea of amateur sailboat racing among the non-moneyed classes, sold for $240 each. Over the winter of 1914–15 the famed Herreshoff shop in Bristol, Rhode Island, produced its first twenty Herreshoff 12½s for a price of $420 apiece. For comparison, a 1915 Ford Model T sedan cost $740. Today you can still buy a basic, factory-produced fiberglass sailing dinghy for half the cost of a cheap new car—in the range of $5,000 to $10,000. But a wooden sailing dinghy worthy of a connoisseur, expertly built and painstakingly detailed, can cost more than *twice* that new car's sticker. An heirloom-quality Haven 12½, the successor to the Herreshoff 12½, starts around $40,000 and ascends through the stratosphere on a steep ladder of options.

Of course I'd rather own the classy Haven than any comparable production boat, just as I'd rather have a mug of freshly ground Starbucks French Roast than Maxwell House. And of course it's always possible that a taste for better things can be interpreted—often rightly—as affectation or pretension. But I think small boats are by their very nature exempt from the charge. I've never seen a small boat, particularly a boat with sails, that struck me as pretentious. Big yachts are another matter. The dividing line is—well, etched in the retina of the beholder. I think it might be in the neighborhood of a forty-foot length.

I hoped my Zephyr would turn out to look a little more like a carefully crafted boat than the plain-vanilla fiberglass variety, or Thoreau's one-week wonder, although at this point it looked like it could go either way. I suspected Henry wouldn't think much of my intention to spend a year building it. He scorned anything that imposed commitment or confinement on its owner—a schedule, a job, a house that demanded daily labor to support its upkeep. "As long as possible live free and uncommitted," he lectured in *Walden*. "It makes but little difference whether you are committed to a farm or the county jail." His cranky libertarianism and no-nonsense frugality appeal to me on a gut level, but I wonder what civilization would have to show for itself if we all took it to heart. Creating things of beauty generally demands fierce commitment on the part of their creators, and it's precisely these things—Brahms's symphonies, Wright's architecture, Herreshoff's sailboats—that enrich civilization.

But a boat doesn't have to be a masterpiece to simply enrich its builder or owner. This is a comforting thought, and I was indebted to a friend named Vicki Altizer for illustrating it for me.

I'd had no idea Vicki had a boatbuilding episode in her past. She's a few years younger than me, petite and vivacious and strikingly pretty—hard to imagine her flocked with sawdust and spattered with paint. But I was telling her about the Zephyr one evening at a dinner party and she said, "I built a sailboat, too, when I was thirteen."

"A model?"

"No, a real sailboat. I still have it; I took my son out for a sail on Lake Washington last summer."

I asked if I could come over and see it. Of course, she said. A few days later I was at her house in suburban Bellevue, staring in amazement at *Lady Bug*, which Vicki had wrestled out from deep storage in the garage for a daylight viewing. She was a miniature, snub-nosed plywood pram just under seven feet long. She had a square ripstop nylon sail and a varnished closet-pole mast.

The workmanship appeared solid but rudimentary. "I was *thirteen*," Vicki reminded me. But *Lady Bug* was indeed a real sailboat: Vicki used to sail her among the San Juan Islands.

The catalyst, as Vicki related the story, was her childhood neighbor, a "Renaissance man" named Arv Cunnington, who was building a twenty-six-foot Thunderbird-class sailboat in his garage next door. Vicki's parents both worked, and she disliked coming home after school to an empty house, so she began hanging out in Arv's garage, watching him work. One afternoon she confided that she wished she had a little boat that she could use by herself at her family's summer property in the San Juans. It wasn't about the water, but the allure of a small swatch of independence. At her age, driving her parents' motorboat by herself was out of the question.

"I've got plans for a little sailboat," Arv said. "I'll show you."

Arv pulled out the plans from a closet. Vicki was struck by how similar they looked to sewing patterns—and at thirteen, she was already an accomplished seamstress. She asked Arv to go over all the materials the boat would require, and she scribbled a list. A few days later, pointedly neglecting to inform Arv or any other adult, she gathered up her hoarded babysitting revenue, enlisted her older brother to drive her to a marine supply store, and trundled back to Arv's garage with $69 worth of marine plywood, fiberglass tape, epoxy, and assorted bits of hardware.

Thirty-five years later, Arv recalled that moment vividly. "I was astonished," he told me on the phone. "Children's pipe dreams are generally transitory. But Vicki was a very unusual child. And I was absolutely thrilled."

The work stretched over seven months, which Vicki recalled as one of the sweetest brackets of her life. Word rattled around the neighborhood, and people dropped by Arv's garage to observe and marvel. She enjoyed the attention, but then, inevitably, the gritty reality of boat work threatened to overwhelm her. Arv knew precisely what to do. "He sat me down and told me this was common when taking on any large project, and you just had to persevere through the doldrums," she said. "He broke down what I needed to do in small steps, taking them one at a time. We set a goal of finishing on my fourteenth birthday."

With that plan, Vicki became boatstricken. She collected her first-ever D in school, in geometry, as boat daydreams displaced attention in class. One could well argue, retroactively, that building a boat *is* an education in geometry. Arv, meanwhile, enforced quality control. When Vicki poured white paint over the hull—"I loved short cuts, and I thought it would be faster than brushing"—Arv wouldn't have it. He made her scrape it off and repaint properly.

She aced the deadline. On July 11, 1970, her fourteenth birthday, her father tucked the boat into the bed of his pickup, and a procession of family and friends trucked her to a small lake in north Seattle. *Lady Bug* was christened either with pink champagne or beer—Vicki's and Arv's recollections diverged here—and launched.

I asked Vicki what, on reflection, the successful project did for her. "I was a typically insecure teenager, and now I had really accomplished something—something that had been *my* idea. I really don't believe I ever asked my parents for permission. I just did it. It also gave me a goal, a passion, and a deep feeling of being cared about by members of a community."

But Vicki never became a passionate sailor, never built another boat. Although she still keeps *Lady Bug* close at hand, by the time I surveyed her she was looking slightly decrepit. Vicki confessed the hull leaked, and hadn't been fixed. What had happened to the passion?

"My life changed. I got busy. I've had jobs ever since I was sixteen. Raising my kids is my passion now. But building the boat had an effect on the way I do it. My number one goal is that they feel safe with me—safe to pursue the things they dream about."

She mentioned then that her son, Bentley, thirteen, was interested in boats. "Could he come over and see the one you're building?"

Thoreau's dory, Vicki's pram, and my dinghy (the terms are surprisingly vague and almost interchangeable) had one thing in common: they all were originally forms of workboats that evolved into pleasure boats. In a capsule, that's the history of North American boating at least until the fiberglass revolution. As spare time gradually trickled into middle-class life in the nineteenth and early twentieth centuries, rowing and sailing for leisure occurred to more and more people who lived close to water. Since the nautical world is inherently conservative and respectful of tradition (as I discovered in my initiation to lofting), builders adapted existing boat forms to new uses rather than inventing.

The earliest made-in-America boats of the colonies were birch bark canoes, copied from the indigenous craft of northeastern Indians. These light, swift boats frankly astonished the white settlers, who must have felt more than slightly embarrassed in their heavy, cumbersome rowboats. "In 1605 three laughing Indians literally paddled circles round the lumbering dory paddled by traveler George Weymouth and seven other men," wrote Charles C. Mann in 1491: New Revelations of the Americas Before Columbus. "Not only were [the Indians] faster," John McPhee wryly added in The Survival of the Bark Canoe. "They could see where they were going." The new Americans borrowed the native technology for inland exploration and, predictably, bloated it up—fur traders eventually commissioned Indian canoes that were thirty-six feet long and could float four tons of cargo. In the nineteenth century, the canoe form migrated to England for leisure-class hunting and picnicking, then finally back to America as an all-purpose pleasure craft. Along the way, builders found that canoes, like most small boats, could be built with an astonishing variety of materials. Indians peeled the pliable bark off birch trees, formed it into a canoe shape, then inserted cedar planking and ribs to give it strength. Since then, canoes have been built out of wood strips, plastic, fiberglass, canvas, Dacron, and least elegantly, aluminum.

The peapod, which started out as a Maine lobster boat in the nineteenth century, might have been the canoe's evolutionary offshoot. It had two pointy ends, like a canoe, but it had a far fatter shape for stability and carried a small sail to help get the catch back to market. It was a perfect example of function dictating form, because the lobsterman would typically stand with one foot braced on the gunwale to haul the lobster pot up from the bottom—a trick that would have caused any other fifteen-foot boat to flip like a wooden nickel. It could even be rowed standing up and facing forward, which was what lobstermen needed to do to locate their traps. When commercial lobstering outgrew the peapods, they too morphed into sweet-tempered pleasure boats—"as stable as advertised, and so perfectly balanced you can steer them under sail just by shifting your weight," reported James Babb in *Gray's Sporting Journal* more than a century later.

My boat, too, had a working-class ancestry, although it's a little less savory. The original melonseeds that inspired Devlin's design were used by market hunters in the late 1800s to stalk ducks and other waterfowl around the shallows of the New Jersey coast. Among these hunters' customers were hat manufacturers, and in the 1880s, the craze for lavish plumage and even entire stuffed birds to adorn women's headwear was decimating East Coast avian populations. The carnage led to the birth of the Audubon Society in 1896 and the Lacey Act of 1900, which outlawed interstate traffic of protected species.

More than almost any other implement, boats have always taken specialized forms to fit local needs and conditions. Boats intended for shallow water will have shallow drafts; boats built for rough water will need decks; boats that need speed will carry proportionately more sail—or engine. And boats built for recreation will demand less expert attention than those built for work.

The first fiberglass boats appeared on the American market in 1947. These were two small sailboats, Carl Beetle's twelve-foot Beetle Swan and Ray Greene's sixteen-foot Rebel. It's no exaggeration to say that they ignited a revolution in boating. For the first time in history, small boats became available that didn't cost much money to buy *and* didn't take much expertise and spare time to maintain. It also marked a pivotal turn away from tradition. After this, innovation in boat design, even sailboats, seemed to occur much more rapidly and with little deference to tradition. A modern trimaran more resembles the starship *Enterprise* than it does a classic sloop. The first electric guitar appeared in 1949 and the first transistor radio in 1954, and both these developments, very close in time and spirit to the fiberglass boat, also led to revolutions in popular culture. In each case it's interesting to ponder whether the new technology created the new culture, or whether the culture was already incubating and ready to bust out, just waiting for the right vehicle.

Eight weeks into the Zephyr, my glop phase—epoxy gluing and reinforcing and fiberglass sheathing—was ready to begin. Any real boatbuilder, even an amateur, would scoff at how slowly I was proceeding on such a small boat. But I was consciously using it to work on one of my prime character defects, impatience, and I was making some progress on that front. I could have started this phase four days earlier, but it was on an afternoon when I had just two hours to devote to the boat, and I didn't want to feel the pressure of time.

The glop phase began in my bedroom closet, where I picked out two ensembles of sacrificial clothes. Pants, shirt, jacket, even sneakers—anything the epoxy touched would be instantly ruined, at least for any further role in public appearances. The glop user is also advised to wear nitrile gloves, chemical-hazard safety glasses, and breathe through "a NIOSH-approved organic vapor filter cartridge." And, of course, don't drink the stuff. It seemed an uncomfortable irony of our time, deploying such a vile gumbo to create a sailboat, the most environmentally gracious transportation device known to civilization.

I would be using the epoxy, two to three gallons of it, in two forms. Thickened to a peanut-butter consistency with wood flour (a fine-grained sawdust), it serves as a fiercely tenacious, waterproof glue and filler putty. Later, in the fiberglassing phase, it brushes onto the flexible glass cloth to saturate it and form a very hard, invisible, waterproof skin on the outside of the boat. I had used epoxy and glass cloth to sheathe my wood kayaks inside and out, so I knew what I was in for. It's hard, tedious, messy work. The real hazard, though, would be mental fatigue—getting so bored or complacent that I would rush the job and louse it up.

I dressed in my finest epoxy duds, checked the alignment of the rickety wired-together hull one last time with my tape measure, and mixed a cup of the miracle potion thickened with wood flour. In one three-hour glopfest, I pressed it into all the hull seams and the joints between the three bulkheads and hull. I was a little neater than I had been with the kayaks, perhaps because I'd been screening a mental movie. A year earlier, gathering material for a book about Frank Lloyd Wright, I interviewed an architect named Arnold Roy who had apprenticed with Wright in the 1950s. Roy recalled the time when he was painting the ceiling of the Garden Room at Taliesin, the Wright compound in Spring Green, Wisconsin, and was splattering enamel all over himself. Wright happened by and was appalled at the sight. He took the paintbrush away and proceeded to demonstrate—"Young man, this is the way you paint!"—even though he was dressed, as usual, in an immaculate suit. No paint dripped or splattered. "From that day on, I learned to be a very clean painter," Roy told me. Now, working on the Zephyr in throwaway clothes, I was visualizing Wright—not so much his brush technique, which I knew nothing about, but his attitude of care. His mindfulness, to borrow a buzzword that's maybe slung around too loosely. It seemed to help.

The next afternoon my epoxy felt hard to the touch, so I took out the wire sutures on the starboard side and the transom. I was anxious for the Zephyr to begin to *look* like a boat. As ingenious as the stitch-and-glue method is, a boat in the early stage of construction still resembles a plywood cow tangled in a barbed-wire fence. When the wires were all gone, at least on one side, its lines and surfaces suddenly exuded a breathtaking grace, even in this raw, unadorned state. *I had given birth to a boat!*

My wrist ached from untwisting and cutting the wires, so I didn't continue with the port side just then. I went into the kitchen, whipped up a celebratory snack of chips and salsa, and ten minutes later returned to the garage to admire my work again.

Just aft of the bow, on the starboard chine where I'd removed the wires, there now appeared a yawning chasm, a two-foot-long, quarter-inch wide gash of air and daylight, where the side panel had just torn itself away from the hull bottom.

It was devastatingly clear what had happened: the glop hadn't fully cured, and the torsional force of the curved plywood, which ached to return to flatness, had overwhelmed the glue. And it was my fault. It was November and the temperature in the garage was hovering around fifty. I was using the slow-hardening variety of epoxy because it's more forgiving in its application, but at that chilly temperature it needed two days to fully cure. Intellectually I knew this, but it *felt* hard enough to my cursory fingertip probe, and emotion dumped reason overboard.

There's obviously a place for emotion in building a boat or anything else—if you love what you're making, revel in its look and feel, you're of course going to *care* more deeply about it, and that's a vital component of quality. But it's not the foundation. Name any human endeavor that encompasses both craft and art—cooking, playing basketball, composing music, designing bridges, landscaping a garden, or building a boat—and it's the craft, or technique, that has to come first.

I had so little foundational technique in boatbuilding that it was scary. The only way I could compensate was to research and think through each episode before doing anything rash, then work carefully and methodically and patiently. That way I had a chance of learning on the job without manufacturing a disaster I couldn't fix. I didn't have the luxury of emotion. I already knew I couldn't afford frustration or anger or impatience, and now I saw that I had to stay away from pride as well.

I avoided the garage for three days. I couldn't bear to look at my plywood indictment, and more significantly, didn't know what to do about it. Cutting the entire hull apart, starting over, loomed like an ominous possibility. The new issue of *WoodenBoat* magazine arrived, and in it was an article titled "Building Nimbus: The lessons of a first-time boatbuilder." Dan Nielsen, the author, graciously provided a photo of the actual bonfire onto which he tossed many pieces of the Haven 12½ he built in a twenty-eight-month marathon of error and trial. "At times I felt as though I was building two boats," Nielsen wrote. "I built the centerboard trunk sides twice, built two wooden keels, four garboards, four sheerstrakes . . ."

Well, the Zephyr wasn't going to fix itself, and I finally returned to the garage to ponder it. I realized first that maybe I could have closed up the gap if I had worked on it immediately when I discovered it, because the epoxy would still have been slightly pliable. I'd felt too traumatized to deal with it—another textbook illustration of emotion getting in the way of problem solving.

I finally worked out a plan that would blend brute force with the lavish application of glop. I spent an hour scraping and sanding off the hardened epoxy on the failed seam, then tattooed the hull panels with holes for a fresh round of stitches. I enlisted Patty to push down hard on one of the panels while I laced them with baling wire and tightened each stitch to within a millimeter of its life. It worked, sort of. The gap narrowed from ¼ to ⅛ inch, and I plastered it with petrochemical peanut butter. The boat looked like it had developed a world-class case of acne.

After waiting a long forty-eight hours for the mess to cure, I tried a little experimental measuring and sanding. My patch seemed to be holding things together adequately, and the boat was still no more than ⅛ inch out of alignment in any measurement. But sanding all the epoxy fillers, reinforcements, and epoxy acne throughout the boat was going to be grueling. Epoxy is much harder than wood. I knew from experience with the kayak projects that the first ten minutes of sanding every day would feel good, in a way, because it's honest and tangible work, a refreshing break from the slippery word-juggling I perform at the computer keyboard. But then muscles would start to ache and cramp, eyes would clog with grit, the bedlam of motorized screeching and muscle-powered scratching would become excruciating, and progress would seem to advance at the speed of geology. All this would be accompanied by an immense temptation to do it just barely good enough, the minimum acceptable standard.

Thoreau was dead right about some things, and here is one of them, straight from *Walden*: "In the long run men hit only what they aim at."

CHAPTER 7

GRIT

WITH WINTER CAME THE dogged days of sanding. In the last three weeks of December, according to my daily boatbuilding log, I spent twenty hours pawing and scratching inside the Zephyr's hull with a vast and varied assortment of sandpaper. On past projects I've found sanding a fulfilling, even pleasant job: a rough or uneven wooden form would become a smooth, functional shape right underneath my hands, a direct and tactile act of creation. A clever tone painting from Handel's *Messiah* (which borrows its text from Isaiah) would spin in my head: "The croo-oo-oo-ked straight, and the rough places plain." In this verse, God was instructing the people of Jerusalem to smooth out a highway for the coming of the Lord.

But the Old Testament Jews never had to deal with epoxy, which formed the rough places I had to render plain. It's not like sanding wood. Epoxy is as tenacious as original sin. It wears like the Rock of Ages. Sanding fillets of wood flour–thickened epoxy—the concave fill joints between adjoining panels of the hull and bulkheads—is like sculpting granite with an emery board.

I alternated among four different kinds of power sanders, depending on what needed attention in what kind of cranny, and endless hand sanding. I confirmed one morsel of advice that pops up consistently in amateur boatbuilding articles, books, and online forums: Don't waste your time and valuable electricity with the cheap weekend-handyperson sanders from the neighborhood home-improvement palace. They're toys. You may be *making* a toy—what else can anyone honestly call a fourteen-foot sailboat here in the twenty-first century?—but even a little boat demands big sanding. You need adult tools. The most useful weapon in my arsenal was a Porter-Cable random orbital sander that's about as large, and as unwieldy, as a sixteen-ounce coffee can. Armed with craggy 60-grit sandpaper, it would grind epoxy loudly and aggressively, although it wouldn't nose into the many concavities on the inside of the hull.

The crannies, the chines, and the tricky places where glass cloth sections overlapped all clamored for hand sanding. I had various rubber and wood sanding blocks, but the most effective technique seemed to be to double up the sandpaper and wrap it around two or three fingers. I could lean into the work and apply a lot of force, and make my fingers assume a shape to conform to any given curvature of the surface. I could feel what was happening through the paper, where the lumps and bumps remained. This primitive technique also obviated the prime hazard of power sanding, that I'd grind too quickly through a thin layer of epoxy and into the glass fibers, which would weaken the boat's structure.

None of this qualified as fun.

The power sanders screamed and fogged the air with unwholesome particulates. I knew it couldn't be good to breathe powdered epoxy, considering the dire warnings about letting the glop touch skin. I wore a respirator that made me resemble a dung beetle outfitted for a burglary. The hand sanding mutilated my fingers; they would ache and tingle and even seep blood at the edges of the nails a day later. I had to program a day of rest between hand-sanding sessions to let my skin and muscles recover. Every surface and object in the garage was flocked with a velvet flour that resisted sweeping or dusting because it was so fine—it wafted into the air at even the approach of a broom or brush.

Northwest Indian tribes built wonderful seagoing canoes out of solid cedar logs before white men appeared in the eighteenth century. The native sandpaper was scraps of shark skin. Supplies might have been a little tricky to obtain, but at this stage of my project I envied the Indian boatwrights: no epoxy.

For those three weeks I mostly worked the inside of the boat. On New Year's Day, a double milestone, I started preparing the outside of the hull for its sheath of fiberglass and epoxy (which would be followed by much more sanding). I wavered between conflicting philosophies, which would have a great deal to do with how the boat eventually looked. One school maintains that an infinite amount of sanding is just barely enough. In my bulging folder of boatbuilding articles was a *WoodenBoat* piece by Aimé Fraser that resonated like a sermon on morality:

The Hull Must Be Smooth, Fair, and Clean

That simple statement contains no hint of the hours of dirty, dusty work with filler and sandpaper that will abrade away your fingerprints and leave you unable to raise your arms above your head. Don't give up; keep your eye on the prize. The time and attention you give to fairing will have a profound effect on the boat's looks. . . . Take the effort to make the hull smooth and fair, and even the simplest boat becomes lovely.

Joel White chimed in with a practical consideration: good-looking wooden boats, he maintained, last longer than homely ones:

The boat that gives one pleasure to look at is a great joy, evoking favorable comment from others. This fills the owner with pride, causing him to take extra care with the boat's appearance. More attention is paid to a handsome craft by everyone involved in her care, whether owner or paid professional; her paint and varnish are better kept, dirt and grime are washed away, problems are dealt with as soon as they appear.

But then I happened onto this contrary piece in *Boatbuilder* magazine by Renn Tolman that recommended just "knocking off the high spots" with a power sander, then priming and painting. Tolman wasn't advocating sloppy workmanship simply to get the drudgery over with. He thought it made more sense to leave the excess epoxy on the boat, where it would help hold all the pieces together, rather than grinding half of it into powder to sweep up off the garage floor.

The result is what I call a "five-yard boat"—it looks as good as any molded fiberglass boat from about five yards away.

I thought *both* arguments were convincing, so I decided on a compromise: I would try for a three-yard boat. I knew I didn't want a watercraft so pristine and perfect that it would vicariously wound me every time the hull got dinged on a rock or a dock, but I also didn't want to sail a boat that I'd be embarrassed to claim as my own work. I was beginning to notice that this problem of finding a middle ground between the ideal and the possible, *and* learning to live happily with it, was arising at every stage of the process. It was starting to look like a core teaching of boatbuilding.

Many of the Zephyr's inside surfaces would be out of sight underneath the deck or seats, or hidden by the foam flotation I was planning to pack in at the bow and stern. The outside obviously asked for more care, at least for the area visible above the waterline. If I were building a fast boat I'd want the surfaces below water to be as smooth as possible, too, but the Zephyr would barely outrun an anemone no matter what I might do, so it seemed to be silly to spend days slaving over the bottom of the hull. This seems counterintuitive, but small sailboats are generally slower than large ones. The following is the only morsel of serious sailboat physics you're going to get between these covers, but it's fundamental to boat design and the transcendentalism of sailing, so listen: The top speed (in knots) of a displacement-hull boat—meaning one that has to push the water out of its way rather than climbing onto a plane and skimming over the surface—is equal to the square root of the waterline (in feet) times 1.34. The Zephyr's waterline is only about 12½ feet long. So no matter how much wind might be blowing, water resistance would limit this boat to:

$$\sqrt{12.5} \times 1.34 = 4.74 \text{ knots}$$

Or, in dry-land numbers, 5.4 miles an hour. That's it. Slower than Patty's kayak, *Sea Major*. Slower than a pathetic-class weekend jogger. More evidence that what was painstakingly evolving under my sandpaper truly would be a toy, not a device useful for any practical or explicable function. But I recall kayaking in the San Juans a few years ago on a calm morning—the wind couldn't have been more than a 5-knot whisper—and overtaking a solo sailor lazing on the deck of a little sloop.

"Great day, isn't it," he called out as I passed.

"Great for paddling," I replied. "Maybe not so much for sailing."

"Why do you say that?"

"You're not going to go anywhere fast."

"Why would I want to go anywhere fast?"

I was recalling this as I began to sand the epoxy-crusted hull, also not fast. I probably could have done the entire hull in one day if I had put my regular life aside and worked all that day, relentlessly, on the boat. That's what a real boatbuilder would do. But I couldn't carve out the time, and I wasn't sure I'd want to even if I could have. My attitude seemed best if I could address six to eight square feet a day, about 10 percent of the hull area. I could manage that much in an hour, starting with the orbital and finishing by hand.

Attitude, I was finding, was at least as critical to the boat work as technique. Possibly more so. In my work life on the other side of the garage door, I'd gotten involved in an intense book-editing job, piecing together contributions from a dozen different writers, and it was tough, tiring work. Some afternoons I didn't trudge out to the Zephyr until 4:30—already dark in the vicinity of the winter solstice in Seattle—and I was so fatigued, mentally and physically, that the boat couldn't give me a lift. On those days I tried to do only a short, menial job, something that would be definable progress but so undemanding that not even a distracted simpleton could mess it up. Another morale booster, I found, was to intersperse small, creative jobs into the drudge work of sanding epoxy. This may run counter to Zen principles, but anyone smoothing out the hull of a boat, as far as I'm concerned, wins an automatic exemption from all conventional measurements of moral and spiritual character. Whatever you've got to do to retain sanity, you do it.

I was consistently failing at my resolution, though, to spend ten minutes at the end of the Zephyr work session cleaning up and putting away. The garage was looking more and more like the definition of entropy; the clutter and disorder were beginning to gnaw at the edges of my good attitude—on the days when I had one—and yet I *still* couldn't discipline myself to clean up regularly. It was too much effort, piled onto the end of a too-complicated day. My project seemed to be proving that chaos is in fact the default mode of contemporary life. The only people who seem to be able to keep a lid on it are the obsessive-compulsives. If there were a sane middle ground, you'd think the building of a sailboat could find the way to it.

Making the rudder looked like a pleasantly undemanding after-noon job, so I shut down my writing and editing early on a rainy January day to do it. Devlin had drawn a rudder that resembles a smoothed-out, upside-down Italy, and its curves seemed almost sensuous. A straight-sided, angular rudder would do its job just as well, but a great deal of the beauty of any boat is invested in its curves: the gradual upturned sweep of the sheer, a bow that either thrusts forward in pride or tucks its chin under in humil-ity. (The Zephyr is very humble, as small boats are wise to be.) Devlin provided grid lines on the plan that I simply scaled up on a sheet of plywood, and that made it easy to rough out the rudder's outline. When it came to the curves, though, I realized I didn't have to follow his plan precisely. I drew them freehand, using my wrist and elbow as a compass point. The ends of the curves looked a little jerky where they elided into the straight lines, so I erased and redrew several times until I was satisfied with the rudder's shape.

My rudder's shape.

I'd just customized my boat. Not by installing accessories or choosing a color out of a catalog, but by designing a hand-ful of curves into it that seemed uniquely pleasing to my eye, that related to the radii suggested by my particular forearm and wrist. How many of us get to place such a personal imprint on the devices we depend on? We can customize some of the func-tions and ergonomics of our cars, but only from limited menus provided by the manufacturers. The personalized curves in the rudder were meaningless as a practical issue, and they were such trivial deviations from the plans that Devlin himself would never notice, but they meant something to me. They formed a quiet declaration of independence, a sign that I was beginning to feel a particle of confidence as a boatbuilder.

I cut out the rudder on the bandsaw and smoothed its curves and straights with 60-grit sandpaper. I sealed one side with fiberglass and epoxy; I would do the other side in a couple of days. The okoume literally gleamed under the sheen of the wet epoxy, and I knew from my kayak experience that after some fine-grit sanding and a few coats of varnish it could look almost like a piece of fine furniture. I might have been lurching into a three-or-more-yard boat, but it would have a rudder that would stand up to a three-inch inspection.

After two weeks of bone-wearying sanding I had smoothed every square inch of the hull. It looked good but felt like hell. Les Wallach, an architect friend who cares so much about craftsmanship that he acts as the general contractor for most of the buildings he designs, once told me: "It's good enough when it feels good under your hand." I could run my fingers over the Zephyr's hull and detect miniature craters, epoxy leprosy, every few inches. I consulted my file of boatbuilding articles and learned what I needed to do: more glop, more sanding. Except for the next round, instead of thickening the epoxy with wood flour, which cures into a rock-hard shell, I could stir in something called microballoons, microscopic air-filled spheres, which makes a glop paste that's said to be easier to sand.

On my next weekly run to Fisheries Supply, the prime boat-builders' emporium in Seattle, I bought a tub of the superfine, almost weightless, auburn-colored powder. It was Saturday, and I literally waited in line for a chance to ask Fisheries' resident boatbuilding expert whether the microballoon mixture really would be more manageable.

"It's *much* easier," he confirmed. "The only thing is, it's not waterproof, so if you use it on the outside of the hull, you'll need to brush on more plain epoxy over it."

In other words: A bare plywood hull is too soft and porous to survive the sea, so I needed to sheathe it in fiberglass and epoxy. This hard layer of epoxy is too rough to paint, so I needed to apply a softer layer over it and sand it smooth. Then, because this soft layer is so porous it could absorb water, I had to brush another hard layer over that. And then sand again. And then, maybe, finally, paint it?

I left the store dazed and wondering: Is it possible that building a boat to a three-yard standard really is an exercise in pointless vanity? Or was I squandering much more time than necessary on this phase of construction because I didn't know any better? Both answers seemed completely plausible.

On that very afternoon the newest bimonthly issue of *WoodenBoat* arrived in the mail, and on the regular "Launchings" page was a photo of a lovely amateur-built thirty-foot cutter based on Long Island, New York. The caption reported that the owner-builder started her in 1985 and launched her in 2005 after 30,000 hours of work. I roughed the math in my head: thirty hours a week for twenty years. The only thing that could lead a person to sustain that much energy and determination for so long a time would be the craving for ravishing, ineffable beauty. *Deep beauty*, a quality that transcends all the ordinary measurements of time, effort, and human sanity.

A magazine assignment for a piece on art in the San Juans came up, and Patty carved out a couple of days off to join me for a long weekend in the islands. We do this at least once a year—I devise some kind of story, schedule a few interviews, and build enough free time around the "work" that we can throw our kayaks into what may be the most beautiful and intriguing paddling environment in North America. The San Juans have become a spendy place to visit, but the magazines pay most of the expenses. To an objective onlooker, this probably doesn't look like hard labor.

I'd been so squeezed for time over the past several weeks that I'd laid almost no groundwork for this trip. I knew people in the San Juans, though, and figured they could point me in the right directions. Winging it is an acceptable, if not exactly noble, tradition in journalism. On a Thursday evening we lashed *Sea Major* and *Plankton* to the Subaru and headed out for the San Juan ferry. Thanks to the expense account, we'd booked a rustic waterfront resort cabin in a quiet, great blue heron–infested bay on San Juan Island's west side. The resort is so accommodating that it even provides miniature thirty-inch-wide boat slips where we can park our kayaks—no tedious trundling between car and water every time we want to go out.

In the tiny, single-room art museum in San Juan Island's main town, Friday Harbor, I noticed an exquisite alabaster salmon by a local sculptor, William Weissinger. "He's a lawyer," the museum director told me. "He took his first stone-carving class from us three years ago." I didn't know how he would fit into my story, but I knew I wanted to talk to him.

It's seldom hard to locate anyone who lives on an island, and Patty and I tracked down Bill Weissinger the next morning at a regional stone sculptors' convocation, where he was chiseling a breadbox-sized block of limestone into an Inca god sporting a necktie. It's an outgrowth, he explained, of a theme he'd lately been exploring—"wereties." As in werewolves. He showed me a series of pencil sketches. Out-of-control ties slithered out of drawers like snakes, bent on apparent mischief. "You can see I'm a little conflicted about my roles as attorney/artist," he said.

He didn't look conflicted that morning. He was dressed in black denim and green flannel, and unkempt gray curls of hair wandered out from under his baseball cap. When we shook hands, his palm felt as rough as the limestone he was reshaping. Certainly rougher than mine—I'd hardly found a stray hour to work on the boat in the past week. Weissinger was friendly and articulate, and we talked about his recently blossomed passion for an hour. At fifty-eight—he was a year older than me—he had just realized his ability to create things of beauty.

I asked if he regretted not uncovering his artistic side sooner. "Oh, sure," he said. "But had I done this in my twenties, I wouldn't have been able to bring all the experiences I've had into it. I think that counts for something."

I noted that the work of sculpting is more than a little like boatbuilding, particularly the sanding phase in which I was then mired: both of us were spending many long, seemingly thankless hours on hard, dirty work before an object of beauty could begin to emerge. "At some point in my life," Weissinger said, "I learned how to grind. To just bear down, concentrate, and do it. Spending one hundred hours on a sculpture—I can do that. It doesn't matter that I'm fifty-eight; I'm determined I'm going to make some nice pieces."

Whatever conflicts might have been rattling around behind Weissinger's wereties, he seemed to have resolved the problem of devoting large chunks of his life to creating something that may have no practical significance. Or else he just hadn't *made* it a problem. Bringing a thing of beauty or intrigue into the world requires no further explanation. Emerson said simply: "Beauty is its own excuse for being." This could be as true of a boat as of a sculpture. If it's beautiful, it leaves ripples of pleasure in its wake, enhancing life on earth in some small way. If it's ugly—clunkily proportioned, badly finished, pocked with epoxy leprosy—it's a form of visual pollution, dishonoring human intelligence and squandering the materials that went into it. You can wander the docks at any marina and see examples of both kinds of boats. Or stroll through any city's downtown and see both kinds of architecture. The presence of beauty makes a difference in the quality of life for all of us, not just for the artist or craftsman or owner.

So all that sanding wasn't pointless vanity. Or at least it didn't have to be, if I chose to look at my little boat as a larger responsibility.

But the sanding didn't have to stretch on into infinity, either. This was something else Weissinger's story suggested. Before he discovered stone sculpture he messed around with clay and decided it wasn't right for him. "You can stretch and mold the same piece of clay for years and years and never finish anything. You can't do that with stone. You keep chipping away, it gets smaller and smaller. So you make your decisions and move on."

Chapter 8

Wind Work

When the thought first dawned that I might build a boat, I programmed Google to flash me a daily alert to every news story arising in the English-speaking world that contained the keyword *sailboat*. This had proven to be both enlightening and unnerving. Although Google's tireless sweep raked up only a handful of stories involving boatbuilding, it delivered a vast and astonishing catalog of things that happen to sailboats and the people aboard them. By my tally of the first six months, three out of every four were not good. Of course this statistic was skewed, because a pleasant day's sail doesn't generate a headline. Trouble does. But look at Google's catch from just two typical days:

> *Man, dog rescued from* **sailboat** *stuck off VA beach*
>
> *Man's body found on burning* **sailboat**
>
> *Coast Guard searches for man after empty* **sailboat** *found*

*Vintage wooden **sailboat** sinks in slip*

*Warships sail to aid **sailboat** under attack by pirates*

Patty and I had taken a beginning sailing course at Seattle's Center for Wooden Boats, a nonprofit boat preservation society, the year before I started the Zephyr. But we hadn't sailed since we completed the course, more or less successfully. The waffly qualifier in that sentence explains our conspicuous inactivity. We didn't feel terrifically confident, so we scrounged reasons over the weekends following the course not to take one of the Center's wooden daysailers out. Then came winter and three months of lousy weather, and by spring we knew that our questionable skills had lapsed into near-oblivion. While there aren't many catastrophic things that can befall a simple daysailer on an urban lake in good weather—fire and pirate attacks seemed remote—there were endless opportunities for embarrassment. What if we couldn't get the sails up? Or down? Docking seemed especially intimidating. The Center's sailboats have no auxiliary engines, so we'd learned, more or less, to dock them under sail. Depending on wind direction and the positions of other boats at the dock, this can be a lot like parallel parking—on a hill, without brakes. We could probably handle it in a light 5-knot breeze, but suppose the wind chose to blow at fifteen when it was time to come in. What would we do then? Careen past the boathouse and yell for a valet?

We'd felt like agonizingly slow and bungling learners, and what we needed to learn about sailing seemed mountainous. For each of the six lessons we had been assigned a different instructor. They were all volunteers, and all were competent, dedicated, and remarkably patient, but they often had different ways of explaining or doing things—for example, how to coil and stow the halyards, the lines that raise the sails. Even with exacting repetition I would have had to coil a halyard fifty times over the six-week course to imprint it in memory. Leaving a spaghetti sprawl of line in the cockpit doesn't necessarily invite disaster, but any competent sailor will tell you that it's an *indicator* of a deeper problem: a careless attitude or multidisciplinary ineptitude. Either 'tude could, and frequently does, trigger one of those headlines.

With the Zephyr taking shape in the garage, we knew we needed another sailing course. Another *beginning* course, since without any sailing practice in more than a year we could hardly pronounce ourselves ready for the next level. We also wanted to qualify for chartering bigger boats.

About two dozen sailing schools are sprinkled around Puget Sound. Some offer their instruction over several successive weekends; some compress an entire course into a weekend on board—like foreign language study by immersion, though for obvious reasons sailing schools avoid using that term. On a blustery winter weekend we visited the annual Seattle Boat Show, where several hundred boats and even more vendors fill the vast Qwest Event Center downtown. The hot trend this year appeared to be ski boats with 600-watt subwoofers. Several of the sailing schools had information booths in the show, so it was a good opportunity for us to browse the programs and ask questions.

Greg Norwine, the owner of Windworks, was manning his company's booth. He made a good impression when I asked him what he thought was the key to good sailing instruction. "The first word that comes to mind is 'management,'" he said. "You should have a concise and consistent product for the students as they go along. There are many different ways to do things on a sailboat, and no single one may be the best. By nature, sailing instructors are independent and spirited, and they may differ in what they think is right and wrong. So we spend a lot of time arguing among ourselves, but in the end we come up with *one way* to teach people to do something."

Patty and I also liked Windworks' setup as a one-stop emporium for sailing. It's a school, a club, a charter outfit, and a yacht brokerage rolled into one. It doesn't have any wooden boats in its fleet, but no commercial charterers do—too much maintenance. But if we could pass the Basic Keelboat course, twenty-four hours of instruction split between classroom and water, we'd be able to charter the club's twenty-five-foot Catalinas for daysailing on our own. Three courses further on, we would qualify to sail the luxurious thirty-four-foot French-built Dufour *Frog Prints* for a week.

Norwine once owned a twenty-nine-foot sailboat, back in his native Texas. After he sold it, he said, he joined a sailing club in Galveston Bay and soon noticed an interesting phenomenon: He was sailing just as much, but his expenses had plummeted. When he'd collect a group of friends to go sailing, they'd see him writing a check for the charter and feel guilty and chip in. That had never happened when he'd *owned* the boat. After that, wherever he moved, he'd join a sailing club. Before long it occurred to him that this was a pretty sharp business model. He moved to Seattle and bought Windworks in 1992.

"Here's why it works, both for us and for the members," he explained. "If you charter a boat on the most expensive weekend day—say, a Saturday in August—and then multiply that cost by seventy, that's what it would actually cost you to own that boat for a year. If we have a member who's chartering seventy days a year, I'll call him and tell him it's time to buy a boat. But in fourteen years of business I've never made that call—because nobody's sailing seventy days a year. The national average, even for people who *own* their boats, is about fifteen days."

I asked why. "Say you've got two weeks' vacation. You've still got to use one of those weeks to visit the family in Kansas. On weekends you still have to mow the lawn, the kids have soccer games. If you plan to take your friends sailing on Sunday, you've got to go down to the marina and spend Saturday cleaning the bird poop off the deck. Real life keeps intruding on sailing."

We signed up for Windworks' Basic Keelboat course and paid the club initiation fee, which together drained us of $1,000. It seemed spendy, but what number surrounding boats isn't? When I had projected the cost of building my simple sailing dinghy, I figured I could build her for $1,500. By this point I'd spent $3,138 and I was less than half done.

Basic Keelboat began in Windworks' second-story classroom overlooking Shilshole Bay Marina, a pincushion forest of white masts encroaching on Puget Sound. More than 1,400 boats live here, most of them sailboats. On this April Fools' Saturday, many more owners appeared to be working on their boats—cleaning, varnishing, performing assorted surgeries—than actually preparing to sail. It was an illustrative backdrop for our class. As we got underway with introductions, one of the fifteen students reported in as a "recovering motor boater." Our instructor, Jim Thomson, laughed agreeably and said that last weekend he had skippered a small group from Shilshole Bay to Port Townsend and back on a twin-engine motor cruiser, a round-trip of ninety miles. "I warned them the fuel bill was going to be a little stiff, but they were still surprised when we filled up at the end of the trip," he said. "It was $350."

Over the next three hours, Thomson introduced us to the basic physics of sailing and the mechanics of the boats. He was genial and patient, with silvering temples and eyes the color of sea on a bright spring day. He *looked* like a sailor, only there wasn't a beard or a hint of crustiness about him. Among Windworks' several instructors, we learned he's the one most likely to concoct a midnight emergency on board, like an open seacock valve that floods the bilge with water, to see how well the student sailors would respond. That would come several courses later, not in this one, I thought with relief.

I found that I easily grasped the physics of sailing, how wind flowing across a sail makes it act as a vertical wing, pulling the boat forward through the water. But I couldn't seem to get the hang of even the simplest knot. It's another dimension of that spatially challenged disability that caused me to build the pulley system in my garage three times and still not get it quite right. It's a good thing I'm not a choreographer for the Flying Wallendas.

Afternoon brought our first on-the-water session, and it seemed alarmingly windy. By the time we groped through the painstaking checklist and motored out of the marina with the Catalina 25's eight-horse Yamaha outboard, the wind was blowing out of the south at a steady 20 knots and Puget Sound was frosted with whitecaps. We had different instructors for this round. Mine seemed no less patient than Thomson but less organized in his teaching. Patty was on another boat. Many schools think it's a good idea to split up couples during lessons; it's a bicker contraceptive. My instructor said we should reef the mainsail at the outset rather than hoist it to its full height. "Reefing" means bunching the bottom foot or two of sail around the boom to reduce the sail area so the boat remains manageable in a strong wind. "The rule of thumb is, if you're thinking about reefing, you should be reefing," the instructor said, which struck me as a perfect lodestone of advice: memorable and unambiguous. The problem was that the wind was already too strong for any of us ham-handed students to undertake the reefing procedure, so the instructor did it himself. I watched intently but I was pretty sure I wouldn't be able to repeat it on my own. There seemed to be a lot of arcane steps with lines and hardware whose functions I was unsure of—pull this, hook that, tighten these.

The instructor kept me at the tiller through most of the lesson. Since I wasn't quite a beginner, I didn't have any trouble steering the boat. The three other students aboard were having difficulty making the counterintuitive leap that to turn the boat right, you have to swivel the tiller left. The instructor saw that I was able to keep the boat out of trouble when the wind was behind us—I had a healthy fear of letting the wind snatch the sail on its trailing edge and whip the boom around in an accidental jibe. That's dangerous because if a human body happens to be within the boom's radius, it'll crack a rib or a skull. The other students needed the practice, though, and they weren't getting enough. The instructor was taking the path of least resistance, which I recognized from my own experience in teaching: call on the student who already knows the answer, because it saves you the effort of guiding someone who's stumbling. But it's not the most effective teaching.

On days like this, Puget Sound essentially functions as a geographic wind tunnel, squeezing and accelerating the Pacific breeze between the two mountain ranges straddling it, the Cascades and Olympics. By mid-afternoon the wind was gusting up to 25 knots, clawing and tearing at the sails while the waves heaved and kicked the hull around. It also began to rain. It occurred to me that there may be no human endeavor in which nature can assault a person in more ways at once than sailing. The next morning my body felt like I'd spent the day in a wine press. My arms, shoulders, legs, back, and neck ached fiercely, and a purple bruise the size of a cell phone decorated my thigh where I'd been bracing to hold the tiller against the weather. I felt beaten up and flummoxed. How could sailing be so much work? And why was I doing it, since its main products so far appeared to be anxiety and fatigue? I wondered if I was in love with the *idea* of sailing rather than the reality, and what I was going to do about it.

I had one thing going for me as a beginning sailor: several thousand miles under my butt in a sea kayak. Although there aren't any boat-handling skills that obviously transfer from kayak to sailboat, I'd at least learned to read the water and a marine chart, and I knew the basics of navigation. If a Washington State ferry in my vicinity were to bellow five times, I would know precisely what the signal means: its skipper thinks my dinky boat is in his way, and he's not happy about it.

But I suspected I had a bigger liability stacked against me: an innate physical ineptitude that has dogged me all my life. I'm a distinctly ungifted athlete—short, slow, clumsy, and cursed with tangled brain wiring when it comes to memorizing any sequence of motions. When I was a kid I tried baseball and basketball with humiliating results. I played table tennis and worked hard at it for more than ten years, and by the time I got to college I was actually pretty good. One semester a student from India who lived in my dorm showed some interest in the game, so I taught him what I knew. A couple of months later I entered the all-college tournament and by fate drew him as my first-round opponent. He slaughtered me. Decades later, around the time I was starting to feel reasonably competent in a kayak, I took a friend out on Lake Washington to give him a first lesson. After three hours he could handle the boat as well as I'd been able to after three years.

There's a perfect word for this: *klutz*, which comes from the Yiddish for "wooden block." You mostly hear people using it in self-deprecation, painting themselves as singularly inept. Yet, the objective evidence is that most of us are klutzes at most endeavors, and we sail through life feeling inferior because we're always comparing ourselves to some exalted standard. George Plimpton, who fashioned a unique journalistic career out of trying things like bullfighting and NFL quarterbacking, wrote in his final book, *The Man in the Flying Lawn Chair*:

> Everyone must wonder wistfully if there isn't something other than what they actually practice in their lives (playing in a yacht-club tennis tournament) at which they would be incredibly adept if they could only find out what it was—that a paintbrush worked across a canvas for the first time would indicate an amazing talent. . . . If an idiot savant could sit down at a piano and suddenly bat out a Chopin étude, wasn't the same sort of potential locked up somewhere in all of us?

Actually, no. The one potential locked up inside all of us, I think, is the capacity to *accept* our limitations and live contentedly with them. But most of us never get there because our culture conditions us to want to excel, to win.

On two more successive Saturdays Patty and I completed the Windworks course, and after our final lesson the genial Thomson ushered us into an empty classroom and administered the "Basic Keelboat" final exam, a multiple-choice written test that took about an hour. There were sections on seamanship, rules of marine right-of-way, and diagram questions in which we had to predict the movements of a boat given certain combinations of wind, sail, and rudder. Those were the hardest for me because they required that conceptual shift between two and three dimensions. There was also a section on naming the parts of the boat, and in *that* subdivision I was fully competent: an idiot savant in his element, finally.

To our surprise, Patty and I both scored in the nineties, which meant we were now certified to sail Windworks' Catalina

25s without an instructor aboard. Without *anyone* aboard who might know what the hell he's doing.

The marine weather forecast was pretty decent: sunny, low eighties, north wind 10 to 15 knots. Patty seemed readier than I was; she was preparing for us to stay out on Puget Sound *all day*. I was worrying that the unseasonable May warmth would kick up an onshore breeze in the afternoon, as the sun heated land more than water. I was still thinking like a kayaker: don't *want* no stinkin' wind. The recollection of that 25-knot lesson remained too fresh. The boat was a bear that day, and we didn't feel even remotely qualified to wrestle that much wind without expert help.

I'd proposed an article on our first "solo" to the *Seattle Post-Intelligencer*, so they were assigning a staff photographer to join us. I had asked the photo editor to designate someone who wasn't a sailor himself so we wouldn't feel additional pressure from a knowledgeable critic laughing himself silly at our beginners' bungling. As we arrived at Windworks' charter office I was already second-guessing that tack: might have been smarter to ask for someone who could help out, even at the risk of additional humiliation.

The photographer turned out to be Dan DeLong, who'd had experience with hazardous assignments—he'd gone to Iraq twice to shoot for the *P-I*. But he's no sailor, he assured us. He told us he once got sick on an assignment involving a shrimp boat back East.

Windworks' relentlessly cheerful office manager, Laura Barry, signed us out on one of the twenty-five-foot Catalinas. It was *Serenity*, the same boat that had pitched and lurched me through that first lesson. Serene like Snorto the Bull.

We heaved our gear aboard and begin working the checklist. We had to review everything from the anchor (is it tied to something on the boat?) to the outboard (will it start?). This ate forty-five minutes, during which the wind seemed to rise ominously. I asked David White, Windworks' dockmeister, to help us reef the mainsail in advance. He deftly did it himself while Patty and I fumbled at the confusion of lines snaking about the sail, mast, and boom, pretending to help. We *still* didn't learn how to do it.

With Patty at the bow helping fend us away from neighboring boats, I backed *Serenity* out of her slip—and began pinballing back and forth in the fairway as I tried to get the boat pointed out of the marina. I was trying to move slowly enough that the three-ton sloop wouldn't slam into another boat, but at such a meager speed the rudder didn't have much bite in the water and the wind kept shoving the bow in directions we didn't want to go. White shouted from the dock that I should swivel the outboard to help steer. "I know, I'm trying; it's stuck!" I yelled back. I was fairly sure there was an adjustment somewhere but I was too busy dodging collisions to look for it. I had a sudden and vivid flashback to age fourteen, trying to parallel park for the first time in a manual-shift car: *lurch/stall/lurch/vrrrooom*. Happily, it was a Monday and there weren't many spectators. There was, however, Dan DeLong, who had been lying belly-down on the cabin roof, firing his Canon at my face, documenting world-class buffoonery.

We finally burbled out of the marina and hoisted the sails. The reefed main looked awful; two feet of sail were hanging under the boom like a beer gut spilling over a belt. We thought we should do something about it but didn't know what. The wind was strong enough, though, that the lousy sail wasn't slowing us down. We were sailing!

That Zen-like oneness with nature, that feeling of being in tune with not only the physics but even the spirit of the wind and water, did *not* descend upon us. Seawater did, as waves began to slap over the deck. Patty took the helm while I climbed onto the cabin roof to try to double-reef the sail. *Serenity* was pitching around so vigorously and the sail flapping so fiercely that I was afraid of getting bucked off the boat—and we'd already decided not to practice our dummy man-overboard drills because the water was too rough. I decided the freakin' sail could fend for itself. When I took the helm again, Patty went down into the cabin for a bottle of water. A wave broadsiding our windward beam threw her into the galley so hard I thought she had broken a bone. But she got up, gamely fending off tears, and came back out to the cockpit.

"I think I've got plenty of good pictures already," DeLong suddenly announced. "I'd kind of appreciate it if you could take me back to the marina." I looked at him with dismay, apparently, registering on my face—this meant we'd have to douse the sails and dock the boat an extra time. "Actually, I'm feeling kind of sick," he confessed. "Looking through the lens with all this motion—"

We returned DeLong to the least congested dock in the marina, then considered our next move. I wanted to abort the afternoon. The wind was way beyond my comfort zone. I was tired, confused, worried. Fifteen years ago in Arizona Patty and I had a pivotal moment like this on a volcanic neck 1,500 feet above the desert floor. It had started out as a casual day hike, but near the end the trail had turned into a near-vertical white-knuckle ascent. Fifty feet from the summit I asked Patty if she was having fun. I was being facetious, but she replied "No!" so emphatically that I just decided to tell the truth myself. "Me neither," I said. "Let's go home." Which we did. And on reflection a few days later we realized what a reward it was to have a relationship where neither of us feels any need to posture, to keep going just to save face. I wouldn't trade that for the summit of Everest.

But these circumstances were different. It was painfully obvious that we needed the sailing practice, and waiting for ideal conditions—a 10-knot wind, less than half of what we were now facing—confounds the essential spirit of sailing, which is to work with whatever Nature chooses to provide, within reason. And we weren't actually in danger. It wasn't a storm, and a heavy keelboat like this doesn't capsize in a 25-knot wind with moderate inland waves no matter how ineptly it's sailed. We were just going to look bad and get ourselves whipped.

For the next three hours we thrashed across Puget Sound, trying to apply at least some of what we'd learned and gain a few shreds of confidence. We tacked and jibed, changing directions through the wind, with no mishaps. Then we tried heaving-to—stopping the boat dead by forcing sails and rudder to work at cross-purposes. Again and again, we failed preposterously. *Serenity* determinedly plowed in circles, like a cat orbiting the spot where it's considering a nap.

By mid-afternoon we were fried. We doused the sails and began motoring back to the marina. When we were about a quarter-mile out, the boat took an odd lurch that seemed unrelated to the waves slurping at our bow, and the propeller sounded as though it had taken a gulp of air instead of water. I gave some throttle. *Serenity* didn't seem to move.

For some reason, the obvious explanation didn't register until Patty pointed it out. "I think we've run aground," she said.

We had indeed. I peered over the transom and could study the geography of the bottom, very close at hand. We were a quarter-mile offshore but it was near low tide, and *Serenity* sported a five-foot draft. Once again, I'd been thinking kayak, where three inches is all we need.

Running aground hadn't been covered in the *Basic Keelboat* course, so we figured we'd better ask for advice. Patty descended into the cabin to hail Windworks on the radio. For some reason, nobody answered. She tried calling on her cell phone. No answer. A video involving tugboats, derisive laughter, and check-writing started to coalesce in my head, and I was suddenly very happy Dan DeLong had gotten sick and was enjoying a dry-land assignment somewhere far away.

When we hit bottom it had felt like soft mud, not rocks, so I figured there hadn't been any damage to the boat. If the keel had plowed a furrow, we could maybe back it out the same way. I waited for a wave to lift us a bit, then revved the motor in reverse. No movement. I kept trying. On the third try the boat finally grabbed enough water and began to move. We backed out to safety, then motored timidly to the marina.

"Do you feel as inept as I do?" I asked Patty.

"I'm too tired to feel."

To our relief, David White met us at the fuel dock to help wheedle *Serenity* back into her congested slip. I expected a scolding; he must have observed at least part of our festival of ineptitude from the dock. Instead, he was disarmingly sympathetic.

"That was kind of like learning to swim in the rapids out there," he said.

The next day Patty showed me a bruise on her backside the color of cherries and raisins and the size of a cell phone—a *Serenity* specialty, apparently. We were both walking bundles of aches. They would evaporate in a day or two, but I was concerned that the negative psychological imprint wouldn't.

What if this trajectory of enchantment with boats and the building and sailing of them ended right here, with the thud of an honest admission that we don't like it? Completing the Zephyr would be pointless, clearly. And what then does one do with a half-finished sailboat in the garage? Too big to ignore, too insignificant to donate to a museum, too floaty to tow out to sea and sink.

Maybe it would wash up on the Google beach:

*Mysterious **sailboat** hull turns up in Costco parking lot.*

CHAPTER 9

WOOD WORK

WILLIAM RUCKELSHAUS WAS speaking downtown at a breakfast meeting of People for Puget Sound, an environmental action organization I'd just joined. Ruckelshaus ran the Environmental Protection Agency in the early 1970s, but enjoyed his fifteen-minute nova of fame as deputy attorney general in 1973, when he resigned rather than follow President Nixon's order to fire Watergate special prosecutor Archibald Cox. Now a private citizen and environmental activist living in Seattle, Ruckelshaus still milks a bit of mileage out of his role in Nixon's meltdown. After thanking the group for inviting him, he added, "Ever since I left Washington, I've enjoyed speaking into microphones I can see."

After this token joke, he turned serious. Puget Sound is in real trouble, he said, its salmon and orca populations threatened by a panoply of pollution sources. The most ominous statistic is that we 3.8 million humans now huddled around the Sound will balloon to a projected 5.4 million in 2020. "The pressures are enormous," Ruckelshaus said. "We have to change the way we live and interact with the environment."

I felt a wave of pessimism. Human cultures have demonstrated again and again that we don't change in response to environmental problems until they become head-on crises, and by then a complete ecological or social collapse may be inevitable. The sociobiologist Edward O. Wilson has a theory why: Early in the course of human evolution we became conditioned to care primarily about the issues that affected our extended family and its surroundings, and at most one or two generations of immediate descendants. In an age of small, self-sufficient hunter-gatherer clans, this compact circle seemed like all that mattered to an individual's welfare, so issues that might sink the entire culture in future generations could be ignored. But even before the Industrial Revolution and today's global economy, that was boneheaded. As Jared Diamond documented in *Collapse*, whole civilizations have regularly blundered into oblivion because they made bad decisions about their environment and resource management. All that's different today is that we have the technology to prolong our denial. If we decimate the salmon runs in Puget Sound, we can still fly seafood in from Alaska or Norway—until we foul *their* spawning grounds, or run out of jet fuel.

But Ruckelshaus wasn't ready to give up, and the tagline of his brief speech packed a compelling resonance. "We should not despair," he insisted, "because failure always follows despair."

I pondered that through the rest of the day, though perhaps in confirmation of Wilson's theory about self-centered myopia I wasn't thinking about the health of Puget Sound, but about the boat in my garage. Lately I'd been edging toward discouragement, if not quite despair. The setbacks and doubts were piling on: that terrible first solo sail, the endless sanding, a crush of writing and editing work that had kept me from spending any more than token time on the boat for several weeks, and a flurry of minor mistakes that had me thinking that the Big One was coming, like the seismic tingles that precede a monster quake.

But Ruckelshaus is right: Tell yourself that you're in the process of failing, and it becomes a perfect self-fulfilling prophecy. It's as true in the microcosm of a man building a boat as it is for a region or nation confronting an environmental problem. If you stop caring, then you start merely going through the motions. You cover up, gloss over. In an age of evangelical personal cheerleading, success slogans are trite and ubiquitous, but I recently ran across this thought from Albert Schweitzer, which seems sturdy enough to transcend popular culture: "The great secret to success is to go through life as a man who never gets used up." That would seem to describe Schweitzer's life, and Ruckelshaus's, and what I needed to do to get back on track with the Zephyr.

Patty's unerring weathervane sensed my emotional doldrums, and one evening while I washed dishes she disappeared into her upstairs studio to work on her computer. This was her usual time slot for answering e-mail, but she took more than an hour and wouldn't answer questions later about what she'd been doing. The next morning at breakfast there appeared a custom-made card at my place with a painting of a big square-rigger on the front and a caption that said: "Life is a great adventure—live it up." Inside, she had written: "For the boatbuilder, love of my life."

Boats have numerous parts that casual onlookers never notice because they're so mundane, and that drive boatbuilders nuts because they're so tricky. One of these is the stem, which is sort of a vertical wooden bumper that forms the leading edge of the bow. It's a vital structural piece because it terminates and draws together the sides of the hull, and because if the skipper slams onto a beach or into another boat, the stem takes the hit. It's deceptively difficult to build because it has to gracefully define the long curve of the bow, and attach in some way that never allows water to seep in behind it and attack the wood with hidden rot. Builders of wooden boats have been known to prowl forests for oaks that grew crooked so they could saw one-piece curved stems from the trunks. Since I didn't want to have to learn forestry to build a fourteen-foot boat, I looked for an easier way.

Devlin's plans were clear, but surprisingly stingy with details. He had drawn the stem in profile, but provided no template, didn't suggest what kind of wood it should be, and neglected to show how it was supposed to be attached. Since I had built a kayak stem on *Sea Major*, which so far hadn't fallen off or rotted, I figured I could maybe adapt that technique to the sailboat.

Over dinner I described the stem problem to Patty and explained how I planned to address it.

"Why don't you call Sam Devlin?" she asked.

"I don't think I need to. I think this'll work pretty well."

She didn't say anything in response, but the faint crinkles of concern and disapproval lingered on her face. She was navigating the narrow passage between offering helpful advice and butting in. She didn't want to see me discouraged or overwhelmed, but also didn't want to find herself aboard a flimsy sailboat that's breaking up in rough water because its very amateur builder was too stubborn to ask for help. She mentally reviewed the times *Sea Major* had survived nasty seas and rough landings, and decided to let it pass—for the time being.

The next day I put my bright idea into action. I would create an inch-thick inner stem of thickened epoxy—hardest substance in the known universe—by pouring it into the crook of the V where the insides of the hull met at the bow. After it hardened, I'd trim it into a nice, smooth curve, then make a template and cut an outer stem of oak to mate with the inner stem.

I scissored a temporary mold for the inner stem out of poster board and fastened it in place inside the bow with duct tape. I mixed six ounces of glop, thickened it with wood flour, then poured it into the mold. So far so good, need more glop. I turned to my worktable and mixed another batch. When I returned to the Zephyr, glop was oozing from underneath the tape and forming a river in the bottom of the boat, like molten lava rolling through the main street of Pompeii. I grabbed more duct tape and tried to plug the leak, but of course it wouldn't stick to liquid epoxy.

I was using slow-curing epoxy, which bought me the luxury of not panicking. I had up to an hour to decide what to do before the lava would solidify. Realistically, there were just two options: muck out all the glop and start over, or figure out a way to live with what had happened. Since the bottom of the boat could use some fortification anyway, I decided on the latter. I snipped a couple of strips of fiberglass, layered them over the arroyo of glop, and brushed on more epoxy to saturate them. When it cured, this would all become part of the boat's structure. It would look terrible, but should mostly escape notice under the deck—and it actually would strengthen the hull. Victory, of a sort, wrestled from the jaws of incompetence.

The next day I built a stronger cardboard mold and tried pouring the epoxy stem again. This time several layers of duct tape held back the river, but the weight of the epoxy made the midriff of my mold bulge, as if it were pregnant. I should have predicted this, too; gravity causes endless problems with epoxy. I grabbed some spare rocks from my garden and weighed down the teeming paper dam, hoping it wouldn't breach again. It held, but my improvised solution looked thoroughly ridiculous. What would Devlin think? He'd laugh, groan, or most appropriately pour a bucket of glop over my head.

I let the inner stem cure under its weighted wall for a couple of days, then chiseled away the cardboard-and-tape mold. No question about its strength. Icebergs? Bring 'em on. Now, however, I had to make the exposed outer stem and attach it, a problem that I hadn't actually thought through yet.

I made a rough template of the outer curve of the bow out of poster board, then snipped away at it with scissors until it fit precisely. Then I transferred that curve to a slab of one-inch-thick oak. The board wasn't wide enough to accommodate the whole stem in one piece, so I drew it as two pieces. Then I cut them out with the bandsaw. I'd become reasonably adept with the saw, so I expected my curve to fit to the inner stem as neatly as nesting spoons. It didn't. Daylight streamed through innumerable cracks and crescents. I also realized that I hadn't considered the direction of the grain in laying out the two pieces, so I now had this nice, vivid oak grain running north in one piece of the stem and west in the other.

I could throw these pieces into the scrap pile and start over. Or I could trim and sand until the imperfect pieces worked, and to hell with the mismatched grain.

I hadn't yet thought too deeply about conservation issues regarding my modest boat—how profligate can a fourteen-foot sailing dinghy be?—but there was a startling mountain of scrap wood nesting under my worktable, and I fully believed what Ruckelshaus had preached so concisely and forcefully: that we'd better change the way we live and interact with our environment. In the macrocosm of planet Earth, a single amateur boatbuilder scrapping five board feet of oak makes no practical difference. But could the attitude expressed by the waste be significant? Could the *refusal* to waste make a point, create a ripple effect through civilization?

I have tried making ripples. When we moved into our achingly suburban neighborhood ten years ago, I was dismayed by all the grass lawns, and by all the time, noise, gasoline, chemical warfare, and air pollution invested in maintaining them. In a fit of reactionary protest, I bought a human-powered push mower. The first time I mowed my front lawn, it actually drew a crowd of neighborhood kids, who'd never seen such a contraption before.

"How come your mower doesn't have a motor?" one asked.

I felt a teachable moment coming on. "Because there's only so much gasoline left on earth," I said. "I believe we ought to save it for more important things than mowing our lawns."

The kid stood there for a moment, looking thoughtful. I wondered if I'd successfully implanted the conservation germ. He turned and wandered away. A few minutes later he was back.

"I told my dad what you said," he reported. "He said you're a nut."

It would be nice to report that persistence paid off, and that human-powered mowers gradually spread through the neighborhood, but no. Several homeowners are now using rechargeable electrics, though, which is a modestly positive step. (More positive would be to get rid of all the worthless grass.) But we can't ever predict or quantify the consequences of a proclamation of personal values. All I know for certain is that despair is the wrong route to fixing *anything*.

Eventually, someone may ask about my mismatched stem pieces. It'll be an opportunity to talk about a balance of values: I made an amateur's mistake, I'll say, that detracted from the beauty of the boat, but not its performance or safety, so I chose to use the flawed pieces. And anyway, there may be so many *other* things wrong with the Zephyr that nobody will ever notice the stem.

I doweled and glued the misfits together. The joint was sketchy, and it took a good hour of sanding to make the stem begin to look like a coherent unit. Then I spent an entire Sunday afternoon trimming its curvature with the orbital sander to match the bow. This left only the problem of how to attach it. Since I'd built it unconventionally, there was nothing in any of my boatbuilding books to explain what to do next: I was on my own.

"Why don't you call Sam Devlin?" Patty suggested.

What the hell. I just blurted the truth: "Because he'll tell me I've chosen a ridiculous way to make the stem and that I'll have to throw it away and start over."

"People have told you he's a nice guy."

"Even nice guys tolerate only so much foolishness."

I decided I could chisel a groove into the inside curve of the stem and, with lavish applications of glop, glue and screw it to the bow. It took about five hours to gouge out the groove, a job that I extended over three days. I was working with agonizing delicacy to avoid the disaster of splitting the wood. Finally, the stem seemed ready. I filled its groove with glop the consistency of peanut butter and squashed it onto the bow, then secured it with duct tape. My boat looked worse than either sausage or legislation in progress. But a day later the glop had cured and I removed the tape, then for insurance installed rather handsome bronze screws fastening the outer to inner stem, and filled the angles at the sides with more glop, finally sanding it to smooth and even graceful seams.

According to my log I had spent twelve hours on this still-imperfect piece. But the Zephyr suddenly looked a little more substantial, a little more like a real boat.

A few days later I mailed Sam Devlin a letter. It seemed faintly quaint, this act of sealing a scrap of personal correspondence in a paper envelope and dropping it in a mail slot, but I wanted to include some bits of the story of how I came to be building his boat, and it felt like a more substantial package on paper. It also seemed like the fitting way to approach a builder of wooden boats in the twenty-first century. I asked if I could drive down to his shop near Olympia, some ninety miles from my house in Issaquah, for a conversation. I was a little vague about why. There were a couple of technical issues looming ahead in the construction, and I didn't want to grope blindly through them as I had with the stem. But it was really bigger than that, and I couldn't explain it to a stranger in an introductory letter.

I'd been avoiding Devlin since I started work on his boat. When my freshly glued hull torqued itself apart and presented that ¼-inch gap between the pieces, Patty suggested that I call him to ask what to do. I didn't. Same with the stem issues. When we had gone to the Seattle Boat Show in January there had been a pair of Devlin boats moored at the Lake Union marina. The owner of one had invited us aboard. It was a forty-one-foot motor cruiser that looked like a classic trawler dressed for an inaugural ball. The workmanship looked like what you'd expect to find on a good violin. Panels fit together with immaculate precision. The curved surfaces of the hull, inside and out, seemed to flow together as gracefully as if the entire boat had been sculpted from a single block of wood.

"Sam's around," the owner said. "He'll probably be back in thirty minutes." I studied the cruiser for twenty minutes and slipped out.

I wanted to meet him, but something just as strong was tugging me in the opposite direction. Fear of criticism, disapproval, inadequacy, asking ridiculous questions—a strong tug, all taken together. And thoroughly irrational. What reason would Devlin have to scoff at my half-built boat or my amateur's questions? Part of his livelihood is selling his plans to builders like me. He wouldn't have much of a business if he made a practice of ridiculing our efforts.

I don't dispose of irrational fears efficiently. I mull, sideline, deny, delay, and avoid; but finally, when a decision has to be made, I take it out and flood it with the hard light of rationality. And then, almost invariably, the fear evaporates. But I never seem to take the shortest route—like a sailboat, I have to tack my way upwind. On the surface that sounds like a very clever analogy, but it's actually not good at all. The human mind isn't constrained by the laws of physics: it *can* sail straight into the wind if it's told to. My vectoring is a character defect. In this case it was driven by pride. Vanity. Fear of being found out for what I actually was: an amateur.

Three days after I mailed the letter, the phone rang, and it was Sam Devlin. "Come on down," he said. "I'd love to learn more about your boat."

Devlin's boat works is tucked away on a remote tentacle of Puget Sound ten miles out of Olympia. It's not in a place that tourists would ever stumble onto, nor would they notice anything remarkable if they did. There's a two-story-tall corrugated steel building with a plastic Port-A-Potty parked at its side, and a wooden outbuilding the size of a small travel trailer with an asymmetrical peaked roof. A sign labels the outbuilding as the office. Half a dozen corroding boat propellers and anchors snore on the wooden building's porch, the only picturesque touch in the complex.

Inside the office, the sloping ceiling is encrusted with photographs of Devlin boats, several of them gracing magazine covers. Devlin is a celebrity in the scattered universe of wooden watercraft. There's a computer, a brass nautical clock, a bookcase stuffed mostly with books about boat design, and two beautiful varnished chart drawers stacked with plans.

Devlin was fifty-three, tall, big-boned, and ruggedly built, sporting a compactly trimmed beard and mustache and a blown-out knee that at the time of my visit was facing surgery the next week. It was an old injury; more than three decades ago it provided him with a pass out of the Vietnam draft. He was in obvious pain when I arrived, but as soon as we started talking boats, the tension visibly drained out of his facial muscles and his eyes lit up. The phone interrupted every five minutes with a customer or supplier asking a question. But I had the impression that I wasn't imposing on his time, that he would gladly talk boats all afternoon and through the night. It's his anesthetic, his spiritual center, his life.

I asked why he became a boatbuilder. He said there's no simple answer, that the only way he could explain it was by sharing a series of mental "snapshots" in his history. The first is from age four or five. He's playing in a landlocked skiff in his father's marine store in Eugene, Oregon. The second is a pivotal moment near the end of his senior year in high school. "I was out by a lake near Eugene with my first girlfriend—I was a late bloomer—and this little sailboat came up and beached right beside us. The guy jumped out and asks, 'Can you hang onto my boat?' He had to run into the woods to take a leak. When he finished, he invited us to go sailing with him. I'd never sailed before, and it opened my eyes. I had no idea there was any feeling on earth like that."

The third snapshot is a sensual daydream that sounds too contrived even for bad fiction, but Devlin described it without a trace of embarrassment. "It was 1974, and I was working in Alaska. I was sitting on an 1898 tug reading issue number one of *WoodenBoat* magazine, drinking strong coffee around a smelly diesel oil heater, and I got this picture in my mind: a long workshop, not too much daylight in it, wood shavings on the floor, a fire in a wood-burning stove. There was no phone. It felt calm, peaceful, contemplative. And I saw myself building wooden boats."

He knew as much about wooden boats then as I know now. He had a double degree in biology and geology from the University of Oregon, which wasn't much foundation. He'd built a fiberglass kayak in high school and had once helped a builder in Eugene plank a fishing boat in traditional plank-on-frame construction. What he did know, or at least believe, was that plank-on-frame made little sense in the twentieth century. Instead of trying to update or refine that ancient technology, he looked directly into the *problem*: how to make strong, leakproof, lightweight, beautiful watercraft with the least investment of labor and materials. Nothing in that equation argued for screwing boards onto oak skeletons. Without knowing that anyone else in the world was already doing anything similar, he devised his stitch-and-glue technique.

He learned later that there were other pioneers around the same time and even earlier, stitching and gluing dinghies together. "Since I didn't know anything about what anybody else had done, I just blundered in," he said. "I had no idea it was considered only suitable for dinghies, and as it turns out that *isn't* a limitation. We've built boats up to forty-five feet, and I think we could go up to 150 feet now if we wanted to. This just reminds me that having too much knowledge of an existing technology can be more of a burden than a help."

As we talked, I watched him become increasingly animated— eyes flashing, hands sculpting boat parts in the air for illustration. "Being a boatbuilder and designer is so integral to me that if you took a fire hose and blew that part of me out, there'd be a little bone and rigging left, but not much flesh. It's such an amazing thing to build boats—to take this pile of materials and breathe life into it. It's the most amazing act of creation I can imagine. These things have a spirit. Sometimes it's a malevolent one, but each one is a unique character."

That was my opening. I told him, "I wouldn't say my Zephyr has a malevolent spirit, at least not yet. But I've had a few problems building it."

"I'm not surprised," he said. "My plans are not terrifically documented on how to build these boats. They're not paint-by-numbers. For one thing, there's no way I can address every issue that's going to come up during construction because I can't anticipate them. But the other thing, I want people to become boatbuilders themselves. My life is not enhanced by seeing more Zephyrs sailing in the world. It's enhanced by seeing the light dance in the eyes of my customers when they see that they can create these things."

We got down to my nuts-and-bolts questions. He addressed each one with sketches on the tattered plan I'd brought, or else he drew a detail on a yellow scratch pad, which he ripped off and handed me. He was so patient that I wondered whether building boats, slow classic sailboats in particular, is an occupation that automatically infuses its practitioners with that quality. That could be an auspicious sign for me—wonder how many boats you have to crank out before it takes root? With my final question, he demonstrated his devastating shrewdness as a businessman. I asked where to find the lead shot for weighting my centerboard. "Oh, we'll just give you some," he said, and called one of the men in the shop to bring some in a couple of plastic buckets.

He gave me forty pounds, enough for three Zephyrs.

"Do you have any pictures of your boat?" he asked.

"I brought one," I said. "I have some trepidation about showing it to you."

He laughed. "Let me see it."

I showed him an eight-by-ten print of the Zephyr on its worktable, taken from the bow looking aft. The digital photo

was plenty sharp, and I worried about all the details his professional eye would pick out—the weird fastening of the stem with
its mismatched grain, the questionable fit of the bulkheads, the
bayous of solidified glop still resisting sanding.

"It looks like you're doing great," Devlin said. "When you're
finished, why don't you bring her down here for her launch?"

CHAPTER 10

THE ZEN OF
SCREWING UP

UNLESS YOU'VE DESIGNED, built, repaired, or bought a sailboat, you've never devoted a second's thought to what one looks like below its waterline. Frankly, it's not pretty. With rare exceptions, a full-Monty view of a full-keel sailboat out of water ruins the impression of grace that it had exuded afloat. It now looks bloated, bathtubby, heavy in the hips. But sailboat design works exactly like natural selection in nature. Over millennia, sailboats have evolved the shapes and appendages they need to survive and move most efficiently, nothing more or less. This is a prime reason behind our fascination with them: no other human-made device has so closely paralleled Nature's own process of evolution.

Until I started studying sailboats and pondering plans, it had never occurred to me that a sailing vessel needs anything other than a sail and a rudder to tack its way around the world.

But of course it does. Most of the time a sailboat is not simply running downwind, but is moving at some angle to the breeze—perpendicular or even upwind. If there weren't some force acting underwater to resist that topside wind, the boat would be a chunk of driftwood sporting a skinny branch and a big leaf, always getting itself blown sideways instead of moving forward. Worse, whenever the wind puffed vigorously enough, the chunk would roll and topple over. To avert these unhappy events, large sailboats have deep keels—lead-weighted fins that extend several feet below the centerline of the hull. The water fiercely resists the slab side of that fin from shoving sideways through it, but offers little resistance to the slim leading edge. Thus the thrust that the wind puts into the sail gets translated into forward motion.

Until some 2,000 years ago, sails were square and sailboats mostly traveled downwind. When the triangular sail appeared, probably as an Arab invention, upwind sailing finally became possible, although European ships stubbornly continued to use oars for windward thrust for another 1,500 years. Viking ships were as sleek as giant kayaks; they didn't need keels because the square sail was only hoisted when the wind blew in the direction the captain wanted to go. The ships of the European Renaissance, finally, adopted combinations of sails that allowed better windward mobility, and they necessarily developed deep, heavy keels.

But by the time of North American colonization, more evolutionary improvements needed to happen. Deep drafts caused trouble for working boats that had to navigate the shallow bays and estuaries of North America's East Coast. Keels were obviously impractical as well for small sailboats (like my Zephyr) intended to be launched from a beach. The solution was some kind of *retractable* keel, either in the form of a centerboard (which pivots down) or a daggerboard (thrusts down). Like many innovations in sailboat design, this idea had a foggy and disjointed provenance. Some ancient Chinese small boats had used centerboard-like devices, as had a form of native South American sailing raft, the *jangada*. Still, a British naval lieutenant named John Schank claimed to have invented it while stationed in Boston in 1771. The Brits skeptically fussed and tinkered with assorted forms of retractable keels and eventually gave up. Three American brothers, however, patented a "centre-board" in 1811, and the device quickly became popular in the upstart nation. Besides having a convenient shoal draft, centerboard-equipped sloops could sail rings around contemporary British boats. The slim boards created less drag in the water than the thick keels of the time. A classic British history, Henry Coleman Folkard's *The Sailing Boat: A Treatise on Sailing Boats and Small Yachts* published in 1906, takes special note of a diminutive American sloop named *Truant*:

> The performances of this little vessel in beating to windward and scudding before the wind were astonishing: no English boat of her size could sail so close to the wind, nor run so swiftly before the wind . . . the *Truant* completely vanquished on the river (as her larger sister the *America* had done on the sea) every boat that competed with her.

Most cruising sailboats today use fixed keels, but they are slimmer and more efficient than in the past. Nearly all trailer-launched daysailers employ centerboards or daggerboards.

Devlin designed the Zephyr to have a pivoting centerboard that resides like the meat of a sandwich in a narrow plywood trunk nearly five feet long, planted right in the middle of the boat. I could see its prime drawback from looking at the plan—it was going to be an elephant in the room, blocking the way of anybody trying to move around the boat. I was also advance-worrying the 2½-inch bolt that would pierce the trunk and centerboard, forming the axle on which the board would pivot. No matter how neatly and precisely I made the bolt hole, Lake Washington, three miles wide and nineteen miles long, would relentlessly try to squirm through it and flood my boat. Any kind of hole below a boat's waterline is a standing invitation to trouble.

I decided to make the centerboard trunk out of ordinary Home Depot fir plywood, half the cost of the beautiful okoume I used for the hull. It wouldn't be a stressed member and it would be painted, so quality wasn't a big issue. The centerboard itself seemed to want to be a piece of solid wood, since it would be shaped to a finlike cross-section that would knife cleanly through water. There's a lumberyard practically in my own neighborhood that specializes in cedar—it's the universal siding and fencing material in the Northwest, thanks to its valiant resistance to the nag of precipitation. Pawing through the aromatic stacks, I found a board that was perfect for my needs: no warp, no knots, sixteen inches wide and six feet long. At the checkout counter I babbled to the lumberman about what a beautiful piece of wood it was and what it would become on my boat. I was thinking he'd be impressed because most of the guys who came through here were just building *houses*.

"Total comes to $99.01," he said.

"Ninety-nine bucks for *one board*?"

"It's 'a beautiful piece of wood.'"

Well, so it was. I went to work immediately, cutting out the centerboard's graceful profile on the bandsaw and then planing and sanding its edges into the slippery shape I wanted. Cedar is an elegant wood to work with hand tools and bare hands because it's so soft and buttery. It willingly accepts any desired curve or form, and feels good under the fingers as it's taking shape: a wood born to please.

Then—this created a momentary knot in my gut—I cut a six-by-nine-inch rectangular hole in it, to later fill with Sam Devlin's lead. Without this weight, the centerboard would float in its trunk, refusing to pivot below the hull. Even with the chunky void in it, though, the piece looked beautiful, as good as an actual boatbuilder might do.

A day later as I was rummaging through the scrap woodpile underneath my worktable, I jostled the centerboard, which was propped on its end, leaning against a table leg. The beautiful piece of wood fell over, smacking the concrete floor and opening a three-inch-long crack from the weight hole to the nearest edge.

My "actual boatbuilder" illusion had survived all of twenty-four hours. I'd just made another amateur's screwup, and not by knocking over the centerboard—all that did was expose its fatal flaws, fortunately on terra firma. First, cedar is too soft and light for a centerboard, which has to endure scrapes and batterings in shallow water. Second, I had cut the sides of the six-by-nine hole perfectly parallel to the grain of the wood, which simply invited the cut to extend itself at the first opportunity. These conclusions occurred as I thought through the problem *after* the fact, running my fingers over my ruined cedar centerboard. I could repair the crack with epoxy, but that wouldn't remedy the underlying issue of having used the wrong kind of wood. There really wasn't any choice but to toss the ninety-nine-buck scrap and make another centerboard.

As I cursed my ineptitude, Mark Coté, my neighbor from three doors south, walked into the garage, sweaty from his evening run. Mark teaches math at the neighborhood middle school and has become a good friend in the ten years we've lived here. I've never been to his class but I suspect he's a respected and well-liked teacher. He has an authoritative but friendly presence, a quick wit, and an optimism that contradicts everything you hear about the sorry state of American public schools—he's forever talking about the "wonderful kids."

I showed him my beautiful centerboard, stupid mistake, and bemoaned the $99 I paid for the useless cedar. "You know the 'project rule,' don't you?" he asked. I didn't.

"Work up your best estimate for materials. Multiply by two. Then work up your best estimate for time. Multiply by four."

I generally worked with the garage door open for light and ventilation, so one neighbor or another would drop in almost daily to visit and monitor the progress. With the arrival of summer, Elizabeth, the nine-year-old next door, became my most reliable habitué. Each time she saw me using a new tool (or chemical) she would pepper me with questions about it. Whatever I was doing to the boat, she wanted to try, and I would let her, as long as it didn't involve toxic soup or sharp tools. Her attention span was measured in seconds, so she didn't prove to be much of an actual helper. She was an endless fountain of provocative suggestions, especially concerning the boat's eventual color. We had this exact conversation half a dozen times:

"What color are you going to paint it?"

"I don't know yet. What do you think it should be?"

"Pink."

"I don't know about that. I haven't seen very many pink boats out there."

"Why not?"

I kept failing to come up with an answer.

We also talked about the boat's name. "What are you going to call it?" she asked several times.

"I don't know yet. Do you have an idea?"

"China."

"Why would I name it 'China?'"

"So you can go there on it."

Elizabeth's father, George, is a computer systems analyst whose personal joy is his garden. My front lawn and assorted plantings—I cannot by any stretch call them a "garden"—look ridiculously scrawny and desultory next to his, but George has never uttered a word of criticism. He simply accepts that my values and enthusiasms are different, and whenever he buys a truckload of flowering plants at the nursery, he quietly installs two or three extras in my yard. I thank him, water them for a week or two, then forget about them and they die. He buys replacements, experimenting with ever-hardier species, and the cycle goes on. Thus it will be as long as we live here, apparently. I will never have one iota of interest in gardening and George will never give up. Obviously, when the boat is finished I will owe Elizabeth many expeditions on the neighborhood lake.

Ava, the nine-year-old Bulgarian girl across the street, dropped in to ask if I could help her with a school project. She had volunteered to build a model log cabin for a pioneer diorama, and after she got home a stark realization struck: she had no idea how to build such a thing. I immediately seized on the most authentic (and grandiose) possibility: literally replicate a log cabin with notched and interlocking wooden dowels. I dropped that plan when I realized that I'd be doing most of the work, which I'd enjoy, but it wouldn't yield much of an educational dividend for her. I then came up with the idea to rip a bunch of dowels in halves lengthwise on the bandsaw, which she could glue onto a simple wooden box to simulate the look of logs. All I had to do was sketch her a plan and saw the logs.

We spent a productive hour on it, and she trundled back to her garage with an armload of pioneer cabin parts, ready to go to work. I felt a warm glow at having played an avuncular role in the neighborhood, oddly diluted with a vector of guilt. I'd just dropped everything to help a neighbor kid with a project, and yet my track record for procrastinating on projects involving my own house is immaculate. I'd been delaying building a new surround for the kitchen window for a year. I'd put off wallpapering the bathrooms—$600 worth of paper was snoring in a closet upstairs—for *three* years. This was impossible to explain or justify, other than to say that the latter two projects didn't sound like "fun." That is not an adult excuse, but it's all I've got.

It might explain why the neighborhood had adopted my boat, however. The conventions of suburban life can seem pretty strict, especially in a subdivision like this where the lots are small and the houses are as blandly conformist as sparrows on a wire (forcibly kept that way by the neighborhood association's architectural controls). There isn't much physical space for anyone to outwardly express a large-scale passion such as the one I'd undertaken. Yet those passions exist, as does a remarkable cultural diversity that didn't exist in suburbs a generation ago. On this block alone there are families from India, China, Korea, Bulgaria, and Ireland (and America). Further confounding the old stereotypes, we know each other and respect our cultural and political differences. The neighbors seemed deeply intrigued with this sudden boatbuilding character in their midst—not quite a nut, but someone whose values had taken a visible tack away from the mainstream, breaking out, pushing the personal envelope. It's something everyone yearns to do in some form, but routine and inertia conspire to subvert it—work, the kids, the insatiable demands of all the conventional chores of home and family life. How can one justify building a boat when the fence needs repairing?

Well, it's easy. You simply declare that a boat has greater value in your life than a fence.

Maybe that *is* an adult decision. A few years ago Michael Pollan observed in *The New York Times Magazine* that a majority of Americans now live in the suburbs, and used the occasion for a revisit to the Long Island 'burb in which he had grown up thirty years earlier. What he found there and elsewhere was that the generalizations we used to hold (and cherish) about suburbs no longer apply. They *aren't* monolithic bastions of monotony and conformity, there *is* life on the sidewalks and the streets, and increasingly, the ideas that are reorienting the grain of our entire culture are being generated in the suburbs. Think about it: Microsoft, Google, and Apple are suburban companies, and their people mostly live in the 'burbs.

For a few days in June the work on the Zephyr suddenly became much more public as it moved out to the sidewalk. I made the mast, twelve feet high and slightly tapered toward both ends, out of Sitka spruce—the Cadillac of woods for use in sailboat spars and piano soundboards because of its tight, straight grain and high strength-to-weight ratio. Feeding a twelve-foot stick into a bandsaw to rough out the tapering profile requires extra bodies, and I drafted Mark, George, or Ava's mother, Elena, at various times to hold the protruding end. When it came time to test-plant the mast in the boat, I decided I needed Mark and his math skills. I had to install an oak wedge near the bow to receive the bottom of the mast, then cut a precise square hole in it so the mast would rake back at Devlin's specified five degrees. I felt embarrassed to ask; I worried that Mark would think I slept through high school geometry forty years ago. I didn't want him to project this onto his contemporary teaching, and start feeling useless and dejected. After mulling this for a week I finally decided it was a ridiculous worry, and on a sunny Saturday morning, I rang Mark's doorbell and explained what I needed. "Sounds like a simple trig issue," he said. "I'll be right over."

He practically bounded into my garage. His wife, Claudia, followed with her camera. "I'm going to turn this into a math problem for the kids," he said. He's teaching trig to seventh graders? Now I'm grossly embarrassed. But after I showed him the plan, he said all we needed to do was drop a plumb bob from the mast and measure the five degrees with a protractor. It wasn't not even a *problem*, it was a *measurement*.

We trundled the boat out to the sidewalk so we'd have the sky for headroom, leveled the hull with foam blocks, and raised the mast. Mark climbed up on a stepladder and dropped the bob on a thread. I jiggled the mast until he said we'd hit the specified five degrees, then I outlined the position of the mast's heel where I'd need to cut the hole. Claudia darted around, taking pictures from assorted angles. "I'll have to juice up the problem a little for the kids," Mark said.

I would have felt like a complete and utter bozo, only Mark was having an obvious good time, and a tight knot of neighbors had gathered around to watch the procedure and pepper me with boat questions. It was a vignette that seemed to suggest an optimistic observation: Apart from the mind-numbing architecture and lawn obsessions, American suburbs are becoming what we'd always hoped our cities would be. Here on the sidewalk in front of my house we had community, street life, diversity, and creativity. And, of prime importance to me, enough space to build a boat. Just around the corner was a lake. How much more could one ask?

Later that same day, Patty and I mounted an expedition to a hardwood supplier in Redmond, our neighboring 'burb. The retailer is in an industrial park whose nondescript architecture completely disguises the exotic delights within (just like our residential street). Inside the store, an enticingly rich bouillabaisse of aroma arose from the stacks of oak, ash, cherry, maple, and mahogany. I pawed through a few dozen boards, not really knowing what I was looking for aside from the dimensions. At Patty's prodding, I finally asked for help. The man at the counter didn't know much about boats, but after I explained what a centerboard does, he recommended ash—heavy, strong, stands up well to lateral loads.

We looked through the ash bins together and failed to find a piece fifteen inches wide—we're just not letting many trees grow to that size before harvesting them today—but I told him I could join two narrower pieces together if he could bevel their edges at forty-five-degree angles for me. I still didn't have a table saw, and doing that kind of precise, straight-line work with a bandsaw is impossible. "No problem," he said, and took a long board into a vast, back-room workshop to cut and mill it for me on the spot. In fifteen minutes a slightly warped, rough slab of ash became two immaculately straight boards, planed to my specified ¾-inch thickness and beveled on one edge each for joining. He charged me $40 for the board and $15 for the instant millwork—a world-class bargain in the context of what I'd gotten used to paying for boat parts.

I spent two weeks building the new centerboard. It was a preposterously complicated process for what is, after all, nothing but a slab of wood that slices through the water. First I mated the two pieces with dowels and epoxy, then cut it to shape. Then, because I wasn't very confident of my joinery, I fiberglassed the whole assembly to reinforce it. Then I cut my six-by-nine-inch hole—being careful this time *not* to align any cuts with the grain—and poured in thirteen pounds of Sam's lead shot, locked it in place with epoxy, and sanded it smooth with the surface. By the time I finished, it all looked so smooth and lovely, the sleek blond grain of the ash gleaming through the transparent glass sheath, that I realized it would be a travesty to paint it. Except that early in the process I had scribbled the words LEADING EDGE in red pencil to remind myself which end was which, so they were now immortalized under glass.

I hammered myself for yet another amateur's screwup, failing to think through the process a few steps ahead. But then a conversation with an old friend bubbled to the surface. Bill Herring is my one childhood friend who inexplicably stayed in El Paso, and I sometimes visit him when I fly in to visit my dad. He's now a renowned artist, and, against the towering odds anyone would have laid down during our high school years, a thinker of considerable depth. Last time I was at his house, I was surveying the piles of junked and half-finished canvases in his studio, and a wisecrack seemed in order. "So, Bill—still clueless and directionless after all these years."

He responded, "Once an artist truly embraces waste and mistakes, he's free."

That scrap of wisdom suddenly burst through to embrace my project—the amateur-quality joinery of the hull pieces, the mismatched grain of the stem, and now the LEADING EDGE notice that would slice proudly through the water, in full view of every trout that cares to read it. Of course one can embrace mistakes too readily and wholeheartedly. If Bill were to let his big ones out into the world's light he'd quickly kill his reputation as an artist; and if I let my big ones compromise the integrity of the boat I could kill . . . well, myself and anyone else with the dumb luck to be along for the ride.

The more I considered it, the more I began to believe there is a kind of moral universe of mistakes, and a hierarchy of error existing within it. We have to correct the big ones—those that have the potential to do real damage to ourselves and others. We can embrace the small ones as affirmations of our humanity; they're only embarrassments if we choose to believe they are. But we have to be willing to gamble, within reason, on mistakes of *all* sizes. Without that willingness, as Bill pointed out, we have no freedom to create. And no one who didn't already know how to build a boat would ever build a boat. Think about the implications.

The centerboard trunk went together easily. It's just a box, the first piece of the Zephyr to be composed of actual straight lines and right angles. I fiberglassed the insides before I assembled it to protect against scrapes and water damage, then I did a trial assembly with the centerboard in place, rotating on its axle. It seemed to work perfectly, although I still anticipated a nagging leak where the axle would burst through the sides of the trunk. I took the centerboard out and set it aside for the time—I didn't want its weight in the boat during construction since I would have to keep turning the hull over.

The last step in the centerboard assembly was a big one, the potential for catastrophe—we're not just talking "mistake" now—frightening. I had to cut a slot in the bottom of my boat, two inches wide and fifty-three inches long. The trunk assembly would perch on top of this, and the centerboard would pivot through it into the water.

I'd been dreading this for weeks, but now that the time had arrived I made a conscious effort to shove emotion out of the picture. I drew the slot on the inside of the hull, measured it three times, then grabbed the jigsaw and cut. I was surprised—alarmed, almost—at how detached I felt. Just a carpenter following a pencil line with a saw. When the cutout clattered to the floor I felt the first flush of emotion, relief that the operation was over. I lifted the trunk and tested it in the slot. Not perfect, but happily, the slot was slightly too narrow rather than too wide. I could trim it little by little with coarse sandpaper.

I left the actual installation of the trunk until the next Saturday, when I had a full day to work. It proceeded slowly and literally painfully, as I had to keep corkscrewing my body under the boat to refine the slot and then jiggle the trunk into position on the inside. Finally I glued it in place, snug against the hull on the bottom and two bulkheads on its ends, and planted sheets of fiberglass against its sides and clear across the hull. The boat had now become one integral piece—hull, stem, bulkheads, centerboard trunk, transom—rather than an assembly of parts. It was no longer just a shell, but a machine—a complex device that implies an intelligent management of nature's forces.

All through the evening, I found myself going out to the garage every couple of hours just to stare, in goggle-eyed wonderment.

CHAPTER 11

FAR FROM PERFECT

A BOAT MEMORY FROM childhood, buried so deeply that nine months of immersion in boatbuilding and sailing had failed to stir it, surfaced suddenly.

I am ten years old, and our family—there are just three of us, Dad, Mom, and me—is on its first-ever expedition-scale vacation outside the stifling orbit of relatives in Texas, Oklahoma, and Louisiana. We are in the hamlet of Spirit Lake, Idaho, visiting two friends my parents had made during World War II while stationed at nearby Coeur d'Alene. Northern Idaho is the most beautiful place I have ever seen, although when one's referential baseline is El Paso, a place so desolate that tumbleweeds routinely patrol the city streets, nearly anyplace else qualifies as fetching. I would have been enchanted by a trip to Topeka. Spirit Lake, though, is lovely beyond anything I've ever seen in Texas or its neighboring states. And our friends lived in a house right on the forest-rimmed lake, complete with their own dock and two boats.

One of the boats is a plain little skiff with a small outboard, an everyday fishing boat. The other is a slick red-and-white wooden cabin cruiser about eighteen feet long. I stare hard at these boats, feeling the stir of some sensation so strange and exotic that my ten-year-old vocabulary lacks words to express it. My father's friend, who doesn't have a kid of his own, picks up on it. "Would you like to drive a boat?" he asks.

"Sure," I say.

"Which one?"

I can't imagine that he would trust me with the cruiser—it must be some kind of an adult joke to offer the choice—so I try to keep the ante low. "The little one."

"Why don't you try the cruiser? It's a lot more fun."

My father turns ashen. He's about to quash this bizarre experiment in the bud. I live on a shorter leash than any other kid I know, rarely allowed to move outside tightly circumscribed activities. But Dad and his friend have had a beer or two, and their judgment is fogged, each in a different way. The friend thinks it's a fine idea to send the kid out for a whoopee in his boat. Dad can't navigate a face-saving way out of the situation. He doesn't want to look like a sourpuss, a no-fun hard-ass, in the eyes of his old Navy bud, whom he hasn't seen in twenty years. So in the remarkable vacuum of any real adult supervision, I am installed in the captain's seat of the cabin cruiser, given three minutes of instruction, and next thing I know I am carving a wake across Spirit Lake, alone, in a miniature universe of ecstasy.

A dozen years later, my new bride Patty was visiting our family home in El Paso for the first time, and Dad dragged out an old box of eight-millimeter home movie reels. We screened a few of them to give Patty an inkling of the boy enclosed in the man she'd just married. In one of them was a brief segment of me in the cabin cruiser backing away from the dock, then planing across Spirit Lake. Dad said, "That was about the scariest hour of my life."

I was recalling all this because my father was dying. He was into his nineties, had lived a good, full life, hadn't had a beer in close to forty years. In this latter bracket of decades he has had excellent judgment, and we'd enjoyed a comfortable, if not particularly close, relationship. But now, nearing the end, I didn't know what to say to him. Or what to feel.

Patty and I were drafting a letter to try to reassure him, in writing, that we would take care of his wife, my stepmother, if he happened to die before her. He'd been making himself miserable worrying about her. She was suffering from advancing dementia and was essentially helpless. We reminded him in the note that he had taught me to honor my responsibilities, and that Patty was brought up in the same way. As truthful and well-meaning as we were trying to be, our note seemed inadequate and hollow. Patty said, "Why don't you put down some happy memory—remind him of a good time the two of you had together?"

I stared at the keyboard and screen, drifting away, thinking hard. I tried to will a good time into consciousness. Fragments of memory flickered and disappeared, but nothing coalesced into a form solid enough for words.

"I can't think of anything," I said. It sounded terrible and cruelly unfair to this man, this decent, honest, and gentle man, who had devoted a substantial fraction of his life to preparing me for a run at mine. But it was the truth, at least at that moment.

We sent the letter. The next day I remembered Spirit Lake and the red-and-white cabin cruiser.

I had been working on the Zephyr almost obsessively since I made a fast run to El Paso two weeks earlier and found Dad in rapidly deteriorating condition, unable to sign his name or sit up for more than a few minutes. He and my stepmother were both now enfolded in hospice care, and we were receiving phone reports every day or two from their nurse. There were around-the-clock caregivers to attend to food, medicine, pain management, and other physical needs. Their assisted-living facility was spotlessly clean, quiet, pleasant, and dignified—one of the best I'd ever seen, and its location in low-cost, low-wage El Paso made it affordable. I felt like I ought to rent an apartment nearby and just be there to offer comfort and friendship. But the sick, hollow feeling that arose in my gut every time I returned to my hometown tugged in the opposite direction. I told Patty it was the sheer physical ugliness of the place. She knew better, knew that it was more about the persistent residue of resentment over a stifling childhood.

"No parent ever gets up in the morning thinking, 'Now what can I do to screw up my kid's life today?'" she reminded me. "They all want the best for their kids, and they do their best within the limits of what they know how to do. They're imperfect, so they make mistakes. Just like we do every day."

I was falling into a pattern of waking up at 3:30 every morning to ponder her wisdom mixed with my guilt, braided with the usual slate of work-related worries. Within a few minutes it would all be pinballing so furiously in my head that there was no real choice but to get up. So I was starting my day's writing at three or four in the morning. (One of the dubious blessings of an office in the home is you have a thirty-foot commute to work when you can't sleep.) By two in the afternoon I'd done plenty of the obligatory work, so I would have a good four hours to spend on the boat. I was chronically fatigued; I practically had to drag myself out to the garage. But once I plunged into the work, I'd get invigorated. The worries didn't drain away, but they at least retired to the background. I noticed that the attraction of shelving them for a few hours every day seemed even bigger than the eventual prospect of sailing the boat.

I was finish-sanding the interior in preparation for painting, and fabricating the interior parts. The latter were basic—a crosswise bench seat, which is called a "thwart" in small boats and canoes, and a couple of wooden brackets to position it. They were far from simple, though. Interior boat parts are never easy, because they have to be shaped to fit the curvature and cant of the hull sides. And I wanted to make these fancier than necessary. I had a vision of a gracefully curving cedar thwart that echoed the inflection of the rudder. Much of a boat's organic beauty is invested in its curves, and the seat promised to be easy to shape on the bandsaw.

I bought an unfinished piece of cedar an inch thick and five feet long to make the curved piece of the thwart. It had a small knot, so it was cheap—only $16. I'd decided I had nothing against knots as long as they weren't in a position to subvert a critical piece of structure. I didn't view them as imperfections; they were the geography of the tree. I was also saving money buying an unfinished board. I'd learned that cedar was so easy to smooth out—three minutes with a sander would do it for this piece—that it now seemed silly to pay for factory milling. I hadn't realized this when I picked out that $99 piece for the centerboard.

Periodically I thought about Dad and the projects we'd attempted together before a deep estrangement in my high school years had made cooperation impossible. Neither of us had known much about woodworking, but he had bought a package set of Skil power tools—circular saw, drill, sander—and together we had groped our way through a remodeling of our single-car garage into a rudimentary family room. Without heat or air-conditioning it didn't prove to be much of a "family" habitat, but it turned into my retreat from the torrents of alcohol-fueled criticism I could expect if I hung out in the main part of the house. The project didn't fully qualify as a happy memory, but it helped me realize that despite our vast outward differences, there was more of my father in me than I'd been willing to accept to this point in my adult life. The garage renovation was a big and intimidating job he hadn't known how to do at the outset, as is my Zephyr. He also passed on to me a moral compass firmly locked onto honesty, responsibility, and ethical work. Somewhere in there had been the spiritual lodestone that had helped both of us quit drinking. In the light of all that, our differences didn't seem very important.

I used the empirical method—cut and try, cut and try—to make cardboard templates for the slight curves where the ends of the thwart had to butt into the sides of the hull. I transferred the templates' shapes to the cedar, then used the rudder I had made several months ago as kind of a French curve to complete the outline of my elegant thwart. (Don't those two words combine for a delicious oxymoronic resonance?) I measured the length three times, then cut it out on the bandsaw. Then I sawed a board for the other plank of the thwart. I planned to leave a ⅛-inch gap between them so water could drain off the seat. Finally, I shaped the mounting brackets out of some scrap cedar.

Not *one* of these pieces fit.

One plank of the elegant thwart was ¹⁄₁₆ of an inch too short. The other sported a bum curvature at one end. The brackets nested sloppily in the crooks where the hull pieces met.

I could have made all the pieces fit through liberal bastings of glop. But I was getting thoroughly sick of sanding it, and I also felt I ought to stick with my original plan just to screw in the thwart so it could be removed if it ever needed renovation. If I glopped the gaps, the thwart would become a structural piece of the boat, locked into place for eternity.

I bought another cedar board, smaller and cheaper yet—only $9. It wasn't wide enough to take the elegant curve of its predecessor, but I was starting to feel that the boat needed an infusion of economic reality. Using the badly fitting pieces as almost-templates, I was able to cut and trim their replacements with just enough adjustments that they fit fairly well—almost precisely, in fact. I'd learned the secret to boatbuilding: just make everything twice. One more mistake surfaced as I slicked the thwart with a coat of clear epoxy to waterproof it: the colors of the two cedar pieces, which the epoxy brought out, were radically different. One was the hue of honey, the other ginger ale. But I would not do it over again. The Zephyr would just have to celebrate the ethnic diversity of the cedar forest.

While I fit the seats, Elizabeth popped in for her daily visit, this time with her mother, Pam. Elizabeth opened with her usual question: "What are you doing?"

I showed her the seat, which to her eyes looked pretty much like a couple of plain boards that I'd been fooling with for three days. "Why don't you just finish the boat?" she asked.

I couldn't think of an answer. I must have looked existentially lost, as if she'd asked the meaning of life. Pam stepped in to save me. "Because Larry's a perfectionist," she said.

"Oh God no!" I said, and I practically leaped around the boat pointing out its gallery of mistakes. I wasn't sure whether I was rejecting Pam's label because I didn't deserve it or because I was afraid of it, but either way, I knew I didn't want it.

A few moments later, echoes of the awkward exchange still lingering in the air, I thought of the name for my boat. I'd been considering names for months, trying to find one that somehow encapsulated a story, yet wouldn't sound pretentious or hilariously ironic if we ever had to radio the Coast Guard for help. The best boat name I've ever seen is *Never Again VI*, but its story didn't fit my project. I'd considered *Precursor* and *Perseverance*, but both seemed overly serious for a fourteen-foot dinghy. The Zephyr's name, thanks to Pam's inspiration, would be:

Far From Perfect.

In the summer's air spaces between writing, teaching, dealing long-distance with Dad's care, and work on the boat, I was devouring every book on sailing and wooden boatbuilding I could find. Some were technical, some unabashedly romantic, some chronicled swashbuckling adventures Patty and I would never, ever undertake—crossing the Atlantic in a twenty-seven-foot sloop—and a few tried, always with difficulty, to grapple with some deeper meaning, to elucidate the values somehow embedded in handmade boats. It was those values that I chased the hardest: What were they? And was there a tangible manifestation, or were they something mystical? Not being a mystic, I hoped for the former. Michael Ruhlman offered an exquisite proposition in *Wooden Boats*, his profile of the boatbuilding firm Gannon & Benjamin: "The science and beauty [of wooden boats] were inextricably linked, were perhaps the same thing." But the commentator who made me think the hardest was a Rhode Island boat designer named Antonio Dias, who wrote in a rambling but intriguing book titled *Designer & Client*:

> It may seem ludicrous to expect boats—and pleasure boats at that—to be vehicles for a search for truth. Aren't they toys, conspicuous consumption, status symbols? . . . Twenty-odd years down this path, I must say that I still have reason to doubt this conventional wisdom. I continue to see glimmers

of the transformative powers inherent in boats and refuse to abandon my expectations.

. . . A boat demands investment from us. And I don't mean financial investment. Every boat presents a challenge; that's what makes it seem almost alive. Without care, boats die—and a dying or dead boat is, at the very least, heart-wrenching. The more time we give to boats, the more they thrive—and the strange part is, so do we. They open us to their own rhythms and to those of the waters they carry us over and through. . . .

The phrase that resonated deeply was *open us to their own rhythms*. A sailboat most obviously does this, because in a sailboat we *have* to understand and cooperate with the wind and current; trying to overpower them is patently futile. This can form a template for our full spectrum of relationships with the natural world, if we allow it to. I was beginning to discern tidal rhythms in my boatbuilding project, too—cycles of fatigue and discouragement alternating with optimism and the joy of accomplishment. Permeating them all was the idea contained in the name *Far From Perfect*. It was wry and self-deprecating and would save the trouble of apology and explanation if I ever got to the point of exhibiting her in one of the wooden boat shows, but it also captured a moment of acceptance that could ripple outward from the boat to embrace other things and people.

Which brought me around to my father, once again. Our relationship, fifty-eight years long, had been very far from perfect. We had never been able to pal around like some fathers and sons; our interests and worldviews seemed chasmically different. Neither of us had tried hard enough at the time in our lives when it could have made a difference. But now, near the end, each of us seemed to have accepted that imperfection and made the best of it that we could.

I wrote my grateful notes about the core values he had passed on to me into my boatbuilding journal, which became this book. Fifteen hundred miles away, in a place where no one thinks about boats, he tacked a color photo of *Far From Perfect* beside his bed and showed it off to all his visitors.

CHAPTER 12

GRETA

ON A WARM AUGUST SATURDAY morning Patty and I tossed *Sea Major* and *Plankton* onto the Subaru's roof rack and drove to a beach park just across Commencement Bay from Tacoma. It's our usual launch site for what has become our favorite paddling destination, a long, deep inlet up the south end of Vashon Island. Although we have to cross the east channel of Puget Sound to reach the island—this includes crossing the shipping lanes—the four-mile-long inlet is arguably the loveliest kayaking environment in the region. It's quiet, secluded from wind and waves on three sides, and punctuated with interesting but not pretentious waterfront homes. And there are always sailboats to ponder.

I had a particular one in mind this day: a small, traditional, carvel-planked wooden daysailer whose lines and craftsmanship were achingly beautiful. She was usually parked a couple of hundred feet offshore near, I assumed, her master's home on the inlet, but every time I'd paddled by, a canvas cover had been stretched over her deck. That's smart preservation strategy for any wooden boat that has to snooze in the sun, but I kept hoping to drop by sometime when the owner had been lazy and hadn't covered her up. I ached to see her naked.

And we got lucky this day—she wasn't wearing her smock. For the first time I learned her name, *Greta*, and I was able to peer over the gunwales into her cockpit. She appeared to be as beautifully crafted inside as out. There was a carving on the coaming with the insignia *ƁB* and the notation *US 107*. I thought that might be enough to track down her story, and possibly her owner.

As soon as we returned home I launched an Internet mission, and discovered the daysailer was a classic twenty-foot BB11 designed half a century ago by the Norwegian builder Borge Bringsvaerd. A British website devoted to the marque praised it as "fast and dry, having an easily driven and particularly seaworthy hull form." About 1,200 were built, and the design was so esteemed that many are still being regularly restored, sailed, and raced. There was nothing floating around cyberspace about the individual beauty named *Greta*, however, and I wondered how I could contact her owner. A moment later, it occurred to me: another Saturday, another expedition to Vashon, and a note in a Ziploc bag.

I felt as though I was having serial affairs, sneaking out to meet assorted boats, hoping for a glance under their skirts, leaving my number in hopes of a hookup on a future date. But only traditional boats—made of wood, powered by sails, in forms that have not changed much for centuries. This seemed startlingly inconsistent with my normal compass heading of aesthetic taste. In my occasional day job as architecture critic for the *Seattle Post-Intelligencer* I'm a relentless opponent of nostalgia in architecture, such as the reactionary neo-Craftsman townhomes and smarmy Hansel-and-Gretel cottages local developers are throwing up in the suburbs and selling for $500,000 to inexplicably uncritical buyers. Retro design in cars and appliances doesn't amuse me, and I've never owned a piece of Early American or Spanish Colonial furniture, authentic or replica. I believe good design respects function and reflects the culture of its own time.

How was it that wooden sailboats were getting a pass?

I dug out Kant's *The Critique of Aesthetics* and Santayana's *The Sense of Beauty* and waded into some aesthetic theory for a few hours. Those waters were frigid, and, for me, largely lifeless. I realized the questions *What is beauty?* and *Why do we respond to it?* are too personal and vivid to be considered in philosophical abstraction. The answers don't come from sitting in a darkened study, thinking hard and deep. They're more likely to occur on a hike in the Grand Canyon, or a walk on the beach.

Because it's out there, in nature, that our fundamental sense of beauty is rooted. I think that at a subconscious level, we compare the forms we know in nature to those we see in man-made objects, and react with instinctive pleasure if the object reveals a relationship to a natural form. The Gateway Arch in St. Louis is a perfect example. It soars into the sky with an effortless grace that seems more like a force of nature than a piece of architecture. In fact, it *is* a force of nature: Eero Saarinen, the architect, took its form from the catenary curve, the arc of a chain hanging between two fixed points, and simply inverted it. It's a universal truth, wherever gravity operates.

We respond more readily to the curved line than to the straight. Curves are the fundamental lines of nature, from the curl of a huckleberry leaf to the exotic S of a great blue heron's neck. Rivers carve serpentine paths in accord with a fundamental principle of physics: centrifugal force causes water to accelerate on the outside of a turn, increasing its power to cut away the bank. Rivers are more beautiful and more interesting than human-engineered canals because of these meanderings. It's interesting to consider how Roman architecture blossomed in the third century BC, when builders began using concrete. That gave rise to the arch and vault, which softened the rectilinear severity of earlier classical architecture. Repeating arches, as in the Colosseum, set up a visual rhythm that echoed arrangements of natural forms—scallop shells, ocean swells, or a canopy of tree branches arching over a path—rather than the imposing but uptight architectural form of the Greek temple.

We crave the patterns and textures of nature so deeply today that we try to replicate them in plastics and composites, usually with egregious results. Remember the spackled linoleum on Mom's kitchen counter or the schoolroom floor? That was supposed to insinuate granite. My Subaru, an otherwise commendably honest and forthright car, has swatches of inane plastic wood framing the center console. It's a vestige of the "woody" craze a half-century back, when station wagons were encrusted with side panels of wood—first real, then fake—that had absolutely no functional value. What car manufacturers are trying to do is convince us that these mechanical contrivances are not entirely divorced from the natural world, and effect some link to the history of wheeled transportation, when wagons and coaches *were* made of wood.

I'm analyzing my own emotional responses to sailboats, and here's what I'm thinking: These creations combine some of the most compelling, elemental forms of the natural world—the curve, the fin, the wing—with just enough outwardly visible mechanical complexity to reassure us that human ingenuity has a rightful place in the gearworks of nature. This connection seems urgently needed if we're ever going to reach that equilibrium in which we consume resources at a sustainable pace and respect nature enough to act like members of a community instead of lords of the manor. We won't achieve that balance by repudiating all technology, nor by imagining that we can use it to invent our way out of every ecological crisis. A sailboat is a symbol of some middle ground, something that suggests a future in which beauty, comfort, and economy might all be achievable within the package of civilization.

I'm also convinced that nobody looks at a sailboat as pure aesthetic form. There's a whole storybook of human culture encapsulated in every boat with a sail, and at some level that colors our perception with intrigue and joy—the latter depending on point of view.

The sailboat is arguably one of the four or five most significant inventions in human history, along with movable type, antibiotics, the internal combustion engine, and the personal computer. It enabled the settlement of three new continents and the establishment of global trade and warfare. Less obviously, it represented the first sweeping triumph of science over superstition: think Magellan. This may be why people who have no connection to maritime life still find themselves almost invariably dazzled by sailing ships or images of them. I have a vivid childhood memory of an intricately detailed model Spanish galleon occupying the prime display niche of my great aunt's living room in the not notably seafaring town of Oklahoma City. It was the most prominent cultural artifact in the house—in fact, the *only* one I can recall from this distance.

This is, of course, a white Euro-American point of view. I haven't yet found a romantic print of a sailing ship over any motel bed on the Navajo Reservation, nor in Makah territory on Washington's Olympic Peninsula. A few years ago, when a parade of replica tall ships sailed proudly into Seattle's Lake Washington Ship Canal, a band of Native Americans unfurled a banner to greet Columbus's *Niña*:

OK, YOU'VE SEEN THE NEW WORLD. NOW GO HOME.

Seattle being the unfailingly liberal and PC place that it is, no jeers erupted. In fact, there was a murmur of applause—from us descendants of those damn pilgrims.

Despite these postmodern pricks of conscience, I think most of us see the sailboat as a symbol of liberation. In the seventeenth century it provided an escape from ecclesiastical tyranny in Spain and class oppression in England. Today it appears to offer an antipode to lives oppressed by schedules, deadlines, urban congestion, noise, and clutter. Nearly everyone who sails will tell you that a great part of its joy comes from aligning oneself to the rhythms of nature, the tides, currents, wind, and solar and lunar cycles, instead of to the grid of a calendar and appointment book. (Note that a tidal graph is a curve, while that appointment book is all straight lines.) A sailboat offers relief from incomprehensible technology; everything on it works according to basic and visible physical principles (unless its owner has chosen to encrust it with electronic navigation, autopilot, and other sources of trouble). Your attention is not divided among a clamoring multitude of information and entertainment; everything is focused on the choreography of boat through water and air. Watching a faraway sailboat from shore, moving slowly, a pure white wing slipping elegantly through the breeze, it *looks* like distilled essence of freedom, even if the reality is a crew working like dogs to optimize sail trim or a new owner facing years of crushingly expensive renovations to a rot-stricken tub that he bought in a moment of swoon.

Paul Gartside, a British-born Canadian boatbuilder, encapsulated it with a commendable twinkle of wit in his essay "A Designer Goes Small":

> . . . Boats are more than a means of transport. They are also expressions of ourselves, our dreams and our fantasies. For many of us boats are symptomatic of a desire to escape the burdensome routine of the everyday, to find the life of romance and adventure we were destined for before it all went terribly wrong. For some people, cars perform the same function but boats have always been the stronger metaphor for me. For one thing, a boat will cut you a lot more slack than a car. It doesn't have to get you to work and back each day. In fact, it can serve much of its purpose simply by sitting half finished in the backyard. I can show you several in my neighborhood that have been doing yeoman service for their owners in just

this fashion for many years. Even unfinished, these boats are still representative of dreams.

If *Far From Perfect* was representative of a dream, it was one of those strange and unnerving ones that seems to tumble into infinity, no conclusion in sight. It was now a month away from my self-imposed September 26 deadline, one year from the start date, and I was not going to make it. The earth had whisked 535,000,000 miles through space while I had built two-thirds of a 13½-foot sailing dinghy—not a stellar performance down here.

My excuse was that real life had intruded on the dream: the entangled logistics of my father's decline, article deadlines, irritating but essential domestic chores, and just feeling too tired on too many afternoons to go out to the garage to work. Chaos was decidedly the default mode of most days. One thing I'd learned was that I *shouldn't* attempt boatbuilding on those increasingly common days when I'd gotten up at 4 a.m., mind buzzing with the day's to-do list, and logged onto the laptop. Twelve hours later I would be too fatigued to muster much enthusiasm, or clearheaded thinking, for solving boat problems. That was fertile loam for sloppy work and stupid mistakes.

So I shifted strategy. I abandoned the boat deadline, gave up trying to work on her every day, and set miniature goals for those days I did work—something ridiculously small but achievable in an hour or two. In *Wooden Boats* Michael Ruhlman noted that one of the palpable joys in the traditional Massachusetts shop where he hung out was that "such boats were gratifying to make; you could run your hand over your progress at the end of the workday." That would be true for me even if "progress" were nothing more than a simple cedar brace for the thwart or a little fairer line on the sheer.

Ah, yes, the sheer: the sweeping line on each side of the boat where the hull joins the deck. Aesthetically, it's the most important line on any boat. Its arc establishes the character of the whole design, like the clarinet glissando that opens *Rhapsody in Blue*. A sharply upturned sheer on a small sailboat gives it a look of saucy impertinence. A long, gentle sweep, which is what the Zephyr had, suggests a dignity that makes the boat seem much larger than it actually is. Most contemporary sport boats—the fiberglass bombs that scorch across lakes at 50 miles an hour—exhibit a *reverse* sheer, in which the arc turns downward at the ends of the boat, particularly the stern. Although it echoes the shape of a dolphin, sailboat people almost universally find it vulgar. I suspect it's not the pure form we're seeing, but the culture of speed and commotion it represents.

I was concerned about my sheer not because of its curve, which I liked very much, but because it was time to make the deck and screw it down. The Zephyr has an unusually complete deck and correspondingly small cockpit for a small sailboat, but this would make it seaworthy, stiffening the structure and shedding waves that might clamber over the bow. Attaching the deck might be the most critical operation to date, at least in terms of the boat's appearance. If the sheer were misshapen or the two sides were even slightly out of tune, my boat would look like a baked potato. This was an operation that I didn't dare hurry.

My first miniature goal was to make and attach one of the sheer clamps—a simple 14-foot-long cedar strip that goes on the outside of the hull to provide a meaty platform for the deck screws to sink into. I figured I could do it in an hour. I didn't have any boards that long, so I cut two pieces that added up to 14 feet. I could massage the joint between them with epoxy to hide it reasonably well.

I bent, glued, and screwed the strip to the hull. It added a three-dimensional definition to the sheer line, instantly making the boat look more authentic. And indeed, it took just an hour and didn't strain my mental reserves. It wasn't until the next afternoon, when my mini-goal was to plane the top of the strip perfectly even with the top of the hull, that I saw the mistake. A one-piece strip, following the curvature of the hull, would have applied uniform bending force to it. My two-piece job failed to exert force where the joint occurred, so there was now a slight kink in the curvature of the hull. It was irritating and well deserving of a dope-slap, but the kink was so slight that I quickly judged it not worth the grief of chiseling off the entire sheer clamp and doing it over. In fact, I proceeded to make the other clamp the same wrong way so the two sides would enjoy the same kink.

I wondered if *Far From Perfect* was becoming a self-fulfilling prophecy.

The next job was to lay out the two mirror-image pieces of the deck on six-millimeter okoume plywood like I had used for the hull and cut them out. This was easy because imprecision was more than welcome; I cut out vague shapes at least an inch wider than they needed to be so I would have plenty of margin for error.

I temporarily attached the vague deck to the hull with C-clamps and backed away to admire. *Far From Perfect* was looking both more like a boat and more like her name all the time. But for the first time I could actually envision her as a real sailboat, heeling and bobbing and making that soft, seductive sibilance as her bow carved the water apart. That was something else I was learning about sailing: it's *not* silent. Your ears are giving you just as much information as your eyes: the progress of the boat through water and wind, the creak of mast and other boat parts, the commentaries of cormorants, sea lions, and other marine traffic. It's *all* important, and one more reason to prefer sailing and paddling to motoring, where the clatter of the engine over-whelms everything else.

Enough daydreaming. There was still a lot to be done before the deck could be permanently attached.

On a September Saturday afternoon I rounded up three neighbors to help cart the boat out the sidewalk again, where I leveled it with foam blocks to try fitting the mast with the deck temporarily in place. Yet another amateur's error: Last time I worked on the mast placement I got it canted back at the req-uisite five degrees, but I didn't consider how I would make sure it wasn't leaning to port or starboard. The mast needed to drop through a square hole in the deck to another square hole in a reinforced plate deep in the hull called the mast step. If the two squares happened to be even slightly out of alignment I would have a cockeyed mast.

They were and I did.

A knot of neighbors clustered around, watching this operation. I had the feeling they expected me to know what to do, which I didn't. I had no idea how a real boatbuilder makes sure the mast is pointing straight up, and I couldn't recall any helpful passage in any of the books or articles I'd read. Was it too obvious to mention? As I contemplated, my suburb came through for me: There was a streetlight two doors north of mine. I walked down to it with my spirit level and checked it for verticality. It was right on. All I had to do was adjust the holes in my deck and step until my mast lined up with the streetlight.

"That's how boatbuilders do it," I told the crowd.

Aligning the holes took three hours of chiseling, sawing, sanding, and filling, and by the time I was done both holes were too wide and the mast was poking through the deck about half an inch to the left of the boat's centerline. But it was vertical. The off-center hole seemed like a lesser sin than a listing mast.

A man driving a black Nissan swerved to the curb next to the boat. He had an Australian accent, and I remembered him dropping by last fall to observe the Zephyr's birth. "It's been a year," he said, remembering with remarkable accuracy. "She's really coming along. She's beautiful. But she really looks like one hell of a lot of work."

He drove off. I rounded up another three neighbors, who affably helped cart the boat back inside. I was vaguely troubled by the Australian's last comment. Not that it was at all rude or derisive, but I began imagining what was unsaid: . . . *and hardly worth it.*

A few days after I dropped my card in *Greta*'s cockpit came an e-mail from her owner, who introduced himself as an accountant named Mike Murray. He didn't think my note was bizarre or a breach of etiquette, and he invited me over to Vashon to take a closer look. A few e-mails later, we concurred on a Sunday afternoon a couple of weeks out, which would be his last sail of the season. He'd haul *Greta* out at the island's marina and truck her to his house for dry storage and renovations over the winter. I'd be welcome to come along.

The appointed Sunday was overcast but calm, and Patty and I paddled over to *Greta*'s mooring to wait for Mike. The little sailboat was resplendent—I scribbled the word in a waterproof notebook and gave thanks that English is so rich as to provide such a perfect descriptor. Its Latin root *splendere* means "to glitter," which is exactly what *Greta* was doing, even on this gray day: gathering all the natural light available, processing it through the honeyed varnish of her African mahogany planking, and rebroadcasting it as a lantern-like glow. *Greta* was practically a floating lighthouse. I also noticed, appreciatively, how her thoroughly traditional construction revealed exactly what's inside her, structurally. All along the hull were rows of circular wooden plugs called "bungs" to cover the screw heads where the planks were attached to the frame members. The bungs literally outlined the bones of the boat. The rows were close together, which told me the bones were substantial. I like things that openly express their structure; it helps me to trust them.

Mike paddled up in a plastic kayak. "You must be Larry and Patty," he said. "You can tie your kayaks to her and we'll sail over to the marina."

We clambered aboard. Mike was a big-boned man with a square-cut face, creased with rugged furrows, hair silvering at the temples. He looked like a professor of sailing. He hoisted the main and then the jib, and gave me the tiller—remarkably gracious, since this would be his last date with this beauty for half a year. The sails filled with a light beam breeze, and he began to tell *Greta*'s story. He said he had been looking for a Lightning-class sailboat—a sporty, race-bred centerboard sloop—six years ago when he stumbled onto *Greta* in the San Juan Islands. She was in storage, under canvas, for sale for $1,200. "I pulled up the cover, took one look, and I was totally hooked," he said. "She had the most beautiful butt of any boat I'd ever seen."

Every story too good to be true, of course, is. This wasn't quite like uncovering a pristine '62 Corvette in a clueless farmer's barn. *Greta* was a great buy only for a person with the nerve and resources of Mike Murray. He'd been sailing for decades, had owned a couple of wooden boats before, and wasn't afraid to perform major surgery on them. *Greta*'s deck was thoroughly rotted from water invasion, and he would have to replace it. He also was fortunate enough to live in a waterfront house with a calm summer moorage. *Greta* has a full keel, which makes her impossible to keep in a garage and trailer-launch for a day's sailing. Mike said he always scoops her out of the water for the winter, but it's a once-a-year adventure that requires the help of high tide and the only boat haul-out hoist on Vashon Island.

During Puget Sound's five-month window of generally fine sailing weather, though, he told me he manages quality time with her. "I have a pretty stressful life. I'm working with a partner on a start-up company, so I go into the city and work that job for a couple of hours every morning. Then I spend the rest of the day on a contract job that's been going on for two years now. When I get home on summer evenings, though, there's time for what I call a 'two-tack' or 'four-tack' sail before dinner. I usually go by myself. Some people go for a martini, I go for a sail. The beauty of this boat is that I can have her rigged and ready to sail in ten minutes. I subscribe to a formula I once heard that the time you actually spend sailing is inversely proportional to the size of the boat. This one is perfect for me. When I want to go for a more ambitious sail, I have friends who have bigger boats. That provides all the access I need."

Mike said he was still just as transfixed by her looks as on the day he uncovered her. In fact, he'd lately been leaving the canvas off just so he could stare at her from his living room window. Yes, there was a trace of ego gratification involved, a pinch of impure thought. "Sometimes," he admitted, "sailing her feels like you're arriving at the dance with the prettiest girl in school."

There was just a light breeze from the north off our starboard beam, but *Greta* responded as effortlessly as a wisp of smoke. I steered with a fingertip. Compared to *Greta*, the other small boats I'd sailed were hippos wading through a bog. Clearly, she was more than just a pretty butt.

A lot of things, though, were converging here *because* of her beauty: Mike's quality of life. Our meeting, which seemed like it would grow into a friendship. The pleasure and perhaps inspiration she continually offered to passersby. And her own survival—there aren't many homely or indifferently constructed boats that live to keep giving pleasure after half a century. They get cut apart and thrown away, to no one's great regret.

The impulse that drives us to bring things of beauty into our lives, often making sacrifices for them, has many facets. It's ego, instinct, sensual pleasure, a cultural response, even the gratification that comes from knowing that you're doing good for humanity by being the creator or custodian of something wonderful. I felt all these things sailing *Greta*, and we'd had just a lunch date.

CHAPTER 13

ALULA

"THIS IS PROBABLY THE best thing I've done in my whole life."

Peter Gron, forty-two, was talking about his Arctic Tern, a twenty-three-foot full-keel sloop taking elegant shape beside his home on Gabriola Island, British Columbia. There was no trace of irony or self-consciousness in his voice or expression—he *meant* it.

If my boat had looked like Peter's, I could have said it was the best thing I'd ever done, too. His Arctic Tern and my Zephyr are blood relatives, both being stitch-and-glue designs from the pencil of the same Sam Devlin, but they are kin only in the sense that great blue herons and chickadees belong to the same biological class. He had named her *Alula*, the Arabic name of a star in the constellation Ursa Major that appeared to ancient astronomers as the first leap of a celestial gazelle. *Alula* would sport a Bermuda rig with a thirty-foot mast, a cabin complete with a propane heater and sleeping berths, and enough design seaworthiness that Peter intended to sail into the open Pacific west of Vancouver Island, out of sight of land.

Not only that, his workmanship made my boat look like a driftwood raft lashed together with sea urchin sinew.

Even *Alula's bottom* was unbelievable. Peter had wanted a supersmooth skin to make her more slippery in the water, and also to discourage freeloading sea organisms from attaching to her. So he bought ten pounds of fine copper powder to mix with epoxy and applied ten coats of dazzling metallic glop to the bottom of the hull and keel, sanding between each coat. After all that, he undertook six more rounds of sanding, progressing from 120-grit to 1200-grit sandpaper and finally to rubbing-compound polishing. The boat's bottom looked like a bronze urn. I drew my fingers across it and it felt like the curving cheek of an ebony-finish Bösendorfer grand.

"This is *beyond* meticulous," I told him.

"I don't want to talk about it," he said, visibly wincing.

But his blog, where he's documented (just as meticulously) his boatbuilding project, did offer a snippet of personal reflection. "There were a few occasions where I had to remind myself, 'Dude, this part will be *under* the water.'"

I had met Peter online, following a link from Devlin's website to Peter's, then wrote him an e-note introducing myself and my boat project. He invited me to drop by. It was a complicated drop, involving four hundred road miles, four ferry crossings, and the usual character-building queues at the Canadian border, but it was worth the trouble. Despite his vastly greater ambitions and construction skills, some remarkable similarities in our experiences were helping to explain something about boatbuilding and its effects on a life's inner direction.

Alula was the first boat he had built, but he had embarked with a lot more foundational skills than I had. His whole family built houses, and Peter grew up around tools and building. "There are old Super-8 movies of me pounding nails into a piece of scrap when I was barely a year old," he told me. Although he had a degree in computer science and worked as a freelance programmer, he'd enjoyed wide experience making furniture and houses. Before he started on the Arctic Tern, he built a place to build it—a wood-framed boat shop beside his house in which the ribs curved skyward to meet in a point like a gothic arch, a translucent plastic skin stretched across them. The workspace inside was bathed with diffused sunlight and exuded the serenity of a forest chapel. There was a cast-iron wood stove to transmute scrap wood into heat; no mound of malformed boat parts collected under his workbench as under mine. He had built the chapel in six days. The photos of it on his website, he said, have drawn as many comments and questions as the boat itself.

"It's very important to me that the workplace be a pleasant place to spend time," he said. "I think that a work environment transfers its character to the thing you're building. I know I've done better work here than I would have in a drywalled garage with fluorescent lights. I *hate* fluorescent lights."

He taught himself to sail in his early thirties, and in 1999 bought a scruffy, leaky, thirty-three-foot plank-on-frame sailboat that he renovated and actually sold at a profit after "sailing the paint off her" for two years—a sequence of events probably unprecedented in the annals of wooden boat commerce. I could see that his familiarity with boats had given him a level of confidence that I didn't have, even though we were both first-time builders. He'd made dozens of departures from Devlin's plan, most dramatically reshaping the keel into an airfoil that would actually provide lift when the wind was trying to shove the boat sideways. Shortly before my visit, he had built an experimental mock-up of a bowsprit, the pointy spar that some sailboats extend a few feet out in front of the bow. "I love the look," he said. "It's like the forward-moving energy of the boat can't be contained within the confines of the hull; it wants to flow somewhere—and the bowsprit is pointing where you're going." There was just one problem. Typically, a bowsprit provides an attachment point for the forestay, which then can fly a larger and more powerful jib than if the sail were pinned to the bow. But Peter didn't want to trust it for that purpose—bowsprits can break, and if the forestay were depending on it, that could fatally cripple the boat. The mast would be the next component to go. And he didn't believe in ornamentation. He had constructed a philosophy of boat aesthetics and engineering in which the adjectives "functional," "simple," and "beautiful" formed a kind of tripod, and if any one of the legs were removed, then the other two would collapse. If his bowsprit wasn't functional, then it couldn't be beautiful, and any superfluous piece would also detract from the essential simplicity of the boat. If an actual bowsprit were to be included, it would have to find something to do.

"Then I figured it out," he said, grinning. "It's a good place to hang an anchor—keeps it from scraping the hull. And on occasion I can use it to fly an asymmetrical spinnaker." That's a tricky downwind sail that I was a good five years away from trying on any boat.

We talked in the boat chapel for a couple of hours, trading ideas on design, woodworking and glop-working techniques, and the nature of the boatbuilding obsession. He told me that he used to be a lot more perfectionistic than he is now, which I told him I found hard to believe. "No, it's a practical matter," he said. "I got rid of a lot of it in computer programming. You can work endlessly to perfect a program, but all the time you're doing it the rest of the world is moving ahead, and then by the time you got it done, it would be obsolete."

"That wouldn't apply to sailboats, especially not one you're building just for yourself," I pointed out. "There's no competition, and nothing on your boat or mine is going to become obsolete."

"But you have to decide on a level of imperfection you can live with. If the bar is too high, you'll never be satisfied with what you've done—or never finish it. When I talked to Sam Devlin, he said you have to reach the point where you want the boat out of your life if you're ever going to finish it. I've reached that point. I want to go sailing."

"I had that same conversation with Sam," I said. "Only he said it even more forcefully. He said he has to start hating it."

Peter laughed, his eyes roaming over the best thing he'd done in his life. I couldn't discern any glint of hate, but he did finally admit to some impatience at this point. "When I started, I was telling people it would take two years to build, but I was secretly thinking: I can do this in a year and a half. It's now been two years and I'm still a good ways off. I'm not telling people for fear of future embarrassment, but I'm definitely shooting for next June."

Given his level of obsession and commitment, I thought: I'll be astonished if he makes it. He wasn't entirely in control of his own head. I recalled talking with a friendly builder from California at one of the wooden boat shows Patty and I had roamed around. He had a fetching but not perfect seventeen-foot catboat, a broad-beamed design with a single sail on a mast planted close to the bow. It was the sixth boat he'd built, all as an amateur. He said he kept doing it because it provided a *respite* from stress. "If you go to bed worrying about a problem at work, you'll still be awake at 3 a.m. If you go to bed think-ing about how you're going to make the breasthook tomorrow, you'll sleep beautifully all night. Why? Because it's fun. It's not rocket science. And you're not doing it for a living."

Peter, in contrast, confessed that the Arctic Tern *had* kept him awake at 3 a.m., most memorably when he was working on fairing the hull at the chine—the angle where two pieces join on each side, and the hull shape becomes a sharper V. "The radius and angle are constantly changing as you move forward. It's dangerous."

The afternoon light shaded into evening. Peter closed up the chapel and we adjourned to his house for dinner. It was a small, simple, starkly furnished A-frame. Parts of the kitchen floor were missing. Boat books and magazines were strewn everywhere, like flotsam. He lived alone. It was the domestic arrangement of a meticulous man who had figured out how to compartmentalize and focus his meticulousness on what really mattered to him, which is something that didn't happen to be inside the house.

Over broiled chicken, I asked him the baseline question: Why build a boat?

"I suppose it's a couple of reasons. First, it's constant problem solving, which is something I like. And a boat requires *elegant* solutions to problems, because they're all out in the open. Second, the problems are always changing, and I like the variety. It was a tough slog on the hull, but now I'm really enjoying mocking up the cabin."

I pointed out that these are reasons for enjoying the process, not reasons to build a boat. "It's an irrational act, as we both know," I said. "You already had a boat, and you could have enjoyed solving problems on it."

"But this is *creating* something," he protested. "Adding a special thing to the world."

I chewed on that during the daylong trip home down Vancouver Island and the always-lovely ferry run through the San Juans to the Washington mainland. It was almost satisfying, but not quite. If he were creating something original or desperately needed, like a sculpture park or a vaccine for AIDS, I could understand why he'd said it was probably the best thing he'd done in his life. But a little sailboat of thoroughly traditional looks, intended only to be sailed by its owner/builder? I followed up by e-mail, trying to get him to go deeper.

"What I really should have said is that this is probably the most satisfying, *completest* thing I've done," he replied. "I feel like this is what I was made to do. It challenges me in so many ways and gives such a great feeling of joy, accomplishment, and satisfaction (and frustration and doubt, etc.). And I just plain love boats and sailing. Like you, I think boats are a thing apart from the rest of man's creations and to be actually creating one myself is wonderful."

That wasn't much deeper, and I thought I knew why. We were at the doorstep of one of the most profound and frightening questions in life: the search for meaning in what we do, and by extension what we *are*. How can the building of a boat face the sharp teeth of the existential maw?

There is an answer, but it would take an awesome leap of faith and then a miraculous transformation in society to get there. If Peter's boat—and the growing numbers of others like it—could somehow inspire a general revival of appreciation for quality craftsmanship, not just in boats but in everything from television programming to the construction of houses, then it would be a meaningful act indeed: it would improve the quality of life on earth.

That's a lot to ask of a boat. But asking it is a lot better than looking at the shabbiness of our cities and the expedient disposability of most of the consumer goods that infest our surroundings and concluding: This is it; this is as good as it's going to get.

Far From Perfect was looking ridiculously, pathetically, irredeemably small, like a lasagna you've just baked for dinner and you realize that it can't possibly feed the six guests who are at this moment shuffling up the walk. Part of it was having visited Peter's Arctic Tern, nine feet longer than my Zephyr and looking one hell of a lot more like a serious boat. Another was having just spent three days on a thirty-four-foot Catalina with Patty and four other members of Windworks, our sailing club, lazily meandering south through Puget Sound and cooking and sleeping aboard. It was our first overnight on a sailboat, and it seemed to beat most of the dry-land weekend alternatives we could think of. The owner had mounted a plaque on a teak bulkhead in the cabin: "The Time a Person Spends Sailing is Not Deducted From His Life Span." Wandering through marinas, I found I was able to look at increasingly large sailboats without reflexively thinking: *pretentious*. Patty and I even reopened the distant possibility of living aboard one in a couple of cautiously exploratory dinner conversations.

Most rational considerations argue for smaller boats, not larger ones. As Mike Murray said of his Norwegian beauty *Greta*, there's an inverse relationship between the size of a boat and the time one spends actually sailing it. The operating costs of any boat rise exponentially with size rather than arithmetically. This is because the larger the boat, the more complexities will naturally accrue to it. It will acquire plumbing, heating, electronics, more rigging and sail-trimming controls, maneuvering aids, and since a boat must function as a self-contained world, backup systems for everything important. If it's large enough to have a wheel for steering, for example, it needs an improvisatory tiller stowed someplace near the cockpit in case the steering gears or cables break. At some point the boat becomes a full-time job just to maintain, thus canceling out the main reason many of us have boats, which is to escape the oppression of a full-time job. A couple of years back, Patty and I went sailing with a couple we know who have a nice thirty-seven footer that they live aboard, off and on. I asked about maintenance. "I keep a running list of about five hundred things I'd like to do to her," said the male half of the couple, who moonlights as a physician.

"That's a joke, right?"

"No, there are really five hundred things," he said, looking slightly offended that I could have even *thought* he wasn't serious.

I'm sort of an amateur sociobiologist, so I'm always looking for evolutionary clues to explain otherwise irrational human behavior. I suspect that our appetite for ever-larger cars, houses, and boats is a kind of territorial claim, not unrelated to a male cat manufacturing an aromatic fence around his property to warn rivals away. Owning a boat is sort of like having your own island, with the added advantage of being able to move it around for a change of scenery or weather. The larger the island, the more secure and powerful you feel. A boat that really is a self-contained city-state—large enough to live aboard, sea-worthy enough to sail anywhere in the world—functions as a declaration of independence.

Ever since I read in Jonathan Raban's superb *Passage to Juneau* that my fellow Seattle writer uses his ketch as a "comfortably down-at-heel floating cottage" to which he flees when a bout of serious reading, writing, or thinking is needed, I've had this nagging dream of doing likewise. All I need for my work is a place to park my laptop computer, a sheaf of file folders, and a bookshelf for books of reference and inspiration. (Teak

OK, cherry preferred.) All this could easily be accommodated within the cabin of a thirty-foot sailboat. And couldn't a clever accountant wring a tax deduction out of it?

The fatal flaw in such reasoning—which almost never prevents anyone from trying it anyway—is that the cost of acquiring and maintaining this floating bubble world will require its owner to work harder and longer hours in support of it. Might those hours be happier, though, because of the boat? That had the ring of another question with existential harmonics, and it's more than I could deal with at the moment.

I needed to refocus on the Zephyr. Distracting daydreams and wish lists can do worse than promote procrastination; they can erode your *caring* about the project at hand. That could be a mortal wound to the building of a boat.

Modeling my five-hundred-item friend, I made a list and taped it to the door of a storage cabinet in my garage. It started off as six things I needed to do before finally attaching the deck to the hull—a point-of-no-return step that would render some areas of the boat forever inaccessible. One by one, the list ballooned to thirteen things. The more I did, the more I saw there was to do. It reminded me of the three lost years I spent studying Russian, a labyrinth of grammar in which each complexity branches into several new subcomplexities, ad infinitum. I never became fluent, which might have been the ominous prequel to this boatbuilding venture.

One of the most critical items on the list was to install permanent flotation, something to displace enough water in the hull so that if it got swamped, it would still function enough like a boat to keep its occupants above water. Some builders create watertight air chambers of plywood and fiberglass. Devlin's construction hints said you could even stuff miscellaneous crannies of the boat with old life jackets. But on one of my earliest round-up expeditions to Fisheries Supply I got intrigued by some flotation-in-a-can magic potion, so I bought it, and it had been waiting on a shelf for six months. What you're supposed to do, I gathered, was to construct a temporary form in the boat—cardboard would work fine, I thought—and pour equal amounts of the two chemicals into it. They were then supposed to mushroom into a permanent foam block in the shape of the form. *Now* I read the warning label, and I wasn't sure it was a great idea:

> DANGER! VAPOR HARMFUL. OVEREXPOSURE MAY CAUSE ALLERGIC SKIN AND RESPIRATORY REACTION. EFFECTS MAY BE PERMANENT. CAUSES EYE, SKIN, AND THROAT IRRITATION. COMBUSTIBLE LIQUID AND VAPOR. KEEP OUT OF REACH OF CHILDREN.

I was kind of worried about this. I didn't really know what precautions to take, aside from wearing gloves and opening the garage door so the force of the explosion would be ushered into the street instead of the house.

I mixed a small quantity of the ominous soup in a two-quart plastic bucket. While I stirred it, it started to get warm and expand, like a witches' soufflé. I poured it into my bow mold. There it rose even more rapidly, a lava dome about to blow out the crater. It foamed over the top of the sheer and congealed into a yellow cumulus cloud clumped around the bow. The instructions had warned: AVOID OVERFOAMING. Apparently that's what I had just failed to avoid. But the cloud hardened in fifteen minutes and I discovered I could shape it neatly enough with a small saw and rough sandpaper. The pour in the stern went better—I ran out of chemicals and underfoamed the cavity, which would leave an inch-high air gap between the foam and the deck over it, once installed. That didn't seem like a problem, but what did I know?

The installation seemed successful, but I was nagged by uncertainties about it. How much toxicity is there in the manufacture of this stuff that nobody knows about? And how reliable is it, in the long run? I hate depending on things I don't understand. In a lot of areas of modern life, we don't have a practical choice. I could have built air chambers, which would have taken more time but would maybe provide more of a sense of confidence and accomplishment. On balance, that's probably a worthy tradeoff.

The baleful warning label prompted me to do some research, and further thinking, about the possible unintended consequences of my project.

On the surface, a sailboat appears to be a paragon of environmental virtues, a model of sustainability. But that appearance is more romantic image than fact. Historically, the construction of wooden sailboats gobbled forests at an astounding rate, particularly after they became large and heavy enough to serve as warships and empire builders. Harvey Green, who wrote an exhaustive history of lumber, estimated that a *single* European warship of the sixteenth through eighteenth centuries claimed fifty to sixty acres of trees. Oak trees, prime material for a wooden ship's structural bones, take 150 to 200 years to mature. I was throwing away an appalling amount of wood for the dinky boat I was building. I'd already filled three bulging thirty-three-gallon plastic leaf bags with unusable offcuts from sheet plywood, dimensional lumber, veneer, molding, and dowels. I had managed to give token bits away as fireplace kindling, but most of my neighbors have converted their fireplaces to gas, as I have, or they just don't use them. The rest of my scrap had gone to landfill. As any good carpenter will tell you, waste is a prime hallmark of poor craftsmanship, and I was wasting plenty either from making pieces wrong, or failing to organize my stock so I could find the most efficiently sized piece for each job at hand. As in so many aspects of modern life, technology was abetting my prodigal ways. The bandsaw cuts wood very quickly and easily, so there's little penalty for failing to think through a problem in advance and measure carefully. If I ruin an entire cedar board, there's an endless supply of replacements available within a ten-minute drive. There's an art to overcoming all the technology-powered incentives to disrespect and waste natural resources, and I think that building a wooden boat could be an ideal vehicle to start integrating a new ethic holistically into one's life. But *Far From Perfect* was only showing me how far from that ideal I was.

The fiberglass revolution in boats undoubtedly has spared vast swaths of forest but extracted other environmental prices. If you drive rural roads around the Northwest, particularly on the islands, you'll see old wooden rowboats cheerfully rotting away on lawns or pastures, looking as organically scenic as biodegrading forest logs or driftwood on the beach. Northwest artists even find them to be appealing subjects; rotting boats regularly appear in sketches and watercolors. It seems like a logical and even spiritually correct part of a wooden boat's life cycle: when she reaches the end of her useful days, just leave her out in the rain to be dismantled and recycled by the nag of bugs and bacteria. It may take a couple of decades, but it doesn't register on human senses as junk, like an abandoned mattress or car.

Or a fiberglass boat. Which is what *Far From Perfect* would be, from a hungry bug's point of view. With most of her wood solidly mummified in glass and epoxy, she'll be inedible. And for all practical purposes, eternal. With a little research, I found an estimate of four hundred years for fiberglass's life cycle, but since the formulation is only sixty years old, that's merely an educated guess. A few environmentalists are beginning to worry about the growing heap of ready-for-the-landfill fiberglass boats around North America. But I called an array of local and state environmental agencies, and no one in Washington State seems to have focused on it. I finally reached Wayne Krafft, a solid waste specialist with the state Department of Ecology, who confirmed that there's no economically viable means of recycling fiberglass. "There's really nothing valuable you can create from it," he said. "On the positive side, it really doesn't do any harm in a landfill, either."

I also reached Mark Goodin, an air-quality permit engineer with the Department of Ecology, who said the acetone and epoxy emissions from my garage were unlikely to waft out in concentrations high enough to affect air quality for anyone except me. "The primary concern would be your health and safety," he said. "And if you have neighborhood kids coming by, keep the garage door open and make sure the use of any kind of volatiles happened the day before." The warning labels, he said, mean business.

All this would have been no concern if I could have convinced myself that I was building an heirloom-quality boat, a priceless watercraft that would be maintained and used for generations, as good wooden boats frequently are. (Seattle's Center for Wooden Boats' collection includes a beautiful sloop dating from 1926; it still sails on Lake Union.) But *Far From Perfect* was a learning experience, a practice boat for someone who's starting too late in life to become a master wooden boatbuilder and thus make the world more beautiful and civilized. I wondered: Was my boat just another indulgence that an overstressed planet can ill afford at this point?

Progress on the to-do list dragged and scraped along for several weeks. None of the chores seemed as interesting as the witches' foam, and I didn't attack them with great enthusiasm or speed. The core issue was getting the deck to fit properly, which seemed to demand endless shimming and trimming. I temporarily installed the two-piece deck with clamps and then removed it for more adjustments a dozen times, and each time the fit would improve by 2 or 3 percent. Finally, on a rainy Saturday afternoon I decided: enough already. The sheer seam wasn't quite uniform and the crown of the deck between the forward bulkhead and the bow was a little warped, like an old LP record that spent the afternoon in a hot car, but it would have to do. The danger of terminal frustration seemed greater than the visual offense of minor malformation.

I lathered the sheer clamps with marine caulk. Its label merely warned of cancer and birth defects, which seemed distantly anticlimactic after the prospect of exploding foam. Then I maneuvered the two halves of the deck into place, drilled several dozen holes for bronze screws, and tightened them down. This sounds straightforward, but it was a four-hour operation. Caulk oozed out of the squished-down sheer seam, and I tidied up the excess with acetone (extremely flammable; causes blindness, neurological damage, and death). Then for good measure, I locked everything down in a thicket of clamps and left it for a day.

Just before bedtime, I sneaked out to the garage to rub my eyes over it—the boat had assumed nearly its final form—and my heart sank. Near the bow, the deck distinctly swelled upward, like the suggestive "power bulge" of a Corvette's hood. What, a sailboat with a big honkin' V-8 in the nose? Worse, the starboard half bulged more than the port half, creating another ¼-inch gap between them. Quarter-inch gaps were becoming my signature. How many can a builder finesse, shim up, or disguise before the spiritual integrity of the boat is fatally compromised? Hell, what about its *structural* integrity? When I awakened for my 3 a.m. carnival of worries, these issues tumbled in my head for an hour—messier problems than the ones that were disrupting Peter Gron's sleep over *Alula*, but no different in their effect on one's peace of mind.

At breakfast I told Patty about the bulge. She didn't think it needed to be an issue. "Just let people assume you intended it that way," she said. To some extent, that would work. But Potemkin confidence wouldn't fool Sam Devlin, and I was starting to worry about the day when I would present my efforts to him.

I took the trash out to the curb after breakfast, passing by the boat. Actually, the power bulge looked slightly cool—or it would, if I could at least bring the two halves of the deck into alignment. There appeared to be two possible ways: pry and chisel the starboard half of the deck off and make a whole new one, or apply brute force in the form of lead weights and fiberglass tape.

Brute force seemed the lesser of the two chores.

I put in an abbreviated day of writing, then went out to the garage to lay down the glass and epoxy. It was now November, and the days were growing decidedly less conducive to boat work. The afternoon light was gray and lifeless, it was raining, and the temperature was hovering at fifty. I actively coveted Peter's cozy wood stove and light-bathed chapel—it was morphing into a boatbuilding cathedral in my mental video—but this was likely a metaphorical overlay for a deeper jealousy. What I really craved was Peter's perseverance, the engine in his character that makes him keep after something until it's *right*. It's a commitment to excellence that grows out of a limitless passion for the thing or act being performed. That seemed to be shaded differently from ego-based perfectionism.

It suddenly struck me that Peter was explaining himself more deeply than either of us realized when he blurted that *Alula* was "probably the best thing I've done in my whole life." His boat had become a passion that will define him, demonstrate what he's capable of doing, and most importantly, what he believes in. It's caused him to focus and concentrate at a level that I haven't yet approached.

No one excels at everything, and we all have the privilege of choosing that defining passion. I wonder if the definition of a wasted life is never getting around to making that choice.

CHAPTER 14

QUALITY TIME

FAR FROM PERFECT HAD a sister ship!

One December morning I clicked onto Devlin's website to run off a print of the sail plan, and for the first time there appeared a link to a log of another amateur builder's Zephyr. He'd finished it at the end of summer, just about the time my boat was supposed to slip into the water and didn't. There were photos—it looked alarmingly good—and a rapturous conclusion. "Every time I launch the boat it draws a crowd of admirers," wrote the builder, a man named Joel Bergen. "It is fast, stable, and tracks straight as an arrow. Thanks, Devlin, for designing my dream boat."

I fired off an e-mail. A few hours later he responded in delight. He told me he lived just an hour away, in another of Seattle's outer-orbit suburbs, and aside from an example in

Hawaii, mine was the only other Zephyr he'd gotten wind of. By the fourth sentence of his note he was suggesting a race.

This is one of the ironic curiosities of sailing: even casual enthusiasts always seem hot to race, despite the fact that boats the size of ours are not going to exceed 5 knots—just under 6 miles an hour—under any conditions in which a sane person would sail them. Probably this is because racing a sailboat is truly an exercise of skill and judgment rather than strength, native intelligence, or (at least at our level) the cash one has available to dump into the boat.

It would be some time before I felt ready to race, but meanwhile I had a pile of questions for my brother builder. And of course I wanted to see his boat in person. After a flurry of e-mails we made a date.

I'd also learned just that week that *Far From Perfect* had a whole flotilla of second cousins, most of them plying assorted bays and inlets of the East Coast. Crawford Boat Building, a shop twenty-five miles south of Boston, specializes in producing fiberglass replicas of the melonseed skiff. Brush Creek Yachts, a North Carolina enterprise, makes strip-planked cedar versions. A few amateurs have spun out their own interpretations. None of these is identical to Devlin's design, but most seem to trace their ancestry to a common source: an 1888 plan reproduced in marine historian Howard Chapelle's authoritative 1951 book, *American Small Sailing Craft.*

The melonseed's history is sketchy but intriguing. Chapelle said the first examples appeared around 1882, apparently as a "drier and more seaworthy" alternative to the New Jersey duck-hunting skiffs called "sneak boxes."

Sneak boxes were designed to lie so low in the water that they functioned as floating duck blinds, but this also rendered them unusable in anything but the calmest water. Chapelle called the melonseeds "remarkably handsome." Another historian, Thomas Firth Jones, added that melonseeds were rowed much of the time and then perhaps quietly sculled to sneak up on relaxing ducks. A shotgun of "perhaps 1½ inches bore might have been bolted to the foredeck, and the skipper might have set it off by pulling a string from aft," Jones speculated. Small-craft historian Barry Thomas wrote that although the melonseed was a very capable sailboat—"it would take an extreme set of conditions to knock her down"—its heyday was short-lived because it was "relatively difficult to build" and therefore too costly for a blue-collar boat that suffered constant abuse from muddy boots and hasty push-offs from beaches and marsh banks. It was encouraging to learn that at least one authority thought building them was "relatively difficult"—it made me feel like relatively less of a bozo.

The best discovery was that I seemed to have chosen, altogether by accident, an incredibly lovely, sweet-tempered, and capable craft. Thomas, who built a replica himself, wrote that "I cannot imagine a safer sailing boat, and unlike so many dinky fiberglass boats, [it] has the feel of a large boat." Famed yacht designer Robert Perry, writing in *Sailing* magazine, called the melonseed and its modern replicas "as shapely a little hooker* as you will find anywhere." Roger Crawford, whose shop has now produced more than three hundred of the little hookers, has an unabashed love affair with them that stretches back to 1987. That was the year that an owner of a rotted-out

*At first I thought Perry had just been at sea too long when he reached for this term, but "hooker" is a legitimate word for a type of Irish fishing boat or any old boat. It derives from the middle Dutch *hoeckboot*, fishhook + boat.

melonseed called Crawford's boat shop to ask if he would try to restore it, and against his better judgment, Crawford agreed to take a look. He got himself bewitched by its lovely lines and not only restored it, but also made a mold of the hull, and from that a prototype fiberglass replica. Two years later the replica entered production.

"The decision to take on the challenge of bringing the melonseed skiff into production was based almost entirely on emotion and passion and very little on economics," Crawford admitted. But he found no reason to regret it. "Even though we thought the melonseed just might sail a little beyond average we were totally unprepared for the sensations of speed, seaworthiness, and outright delight that the boat offered. This boat just *loved* to sail. It is a wonderful thing in life when realities live up to fantasies."

Patty and I drove up to Joel Bergen's house on New Year's Eve. I found a portly, amiable man who wasn't exactly enjoying his holiday season. November and December rains, about twenty-three inches in all, had turned his front yard into a suburban swamp, and he was spending the year's final weekend planting an underground drainage system. The fall weather had been so dismal, even by Seattle standards, that he'd only been able to sail *Quality Time* five times since her completion. But the garage door was open as we pulled up, and we could see the Zephyr gleaming in there, perky and eager as a cocker spaniel pup. As soon as we turned to her, Joel's glum drainage-installation face brightened dramatically.

He told me he had spent two years searching for a sailboat, something small enough to stash in his one-car garage and sail by himself, and that had the integrity of a historic design. He stumbled online onto the professionally built melonseeds, and they struck him as just about perfect—except for the price, which edged close to $10,000. "That led me to Devlin," he said.

It was obviously the right move for him. He worked demonically and finished *Quality Time* in four months—one-fourth the time I'd taken to not complete *Far From Perfect*. In an especially dismaying irony, he had finished on the exact day of my original deadline, September 26.

"I was so excited, so pumped up, it just consumed me," he said. "I was literally thinking about it all the time. Sometimes I'd find it difficult to put it out of my mind and concentrate on my job or family matters. I'd typically come home from work around four, take care of family business, have dinner, and work on it from six until ten. On Saturdays and Sundays I'd usually work from dawn to dusk. Building this was the most enjoyable project of my life and I just couldn't get enough of it. I know it probably sounds strange, but it became an obsession—almost an addiction, like a drug."

Cindy, Joel's wife, injected her observations. "We've been married twenty-five years, so we know each other pretty well. I've seen him smile more in the last eight months than any time over the last eight years. He was just glowing over it."

We turned to the boat. I was a little afraid to commence the examination because Joel's obviously successful project might be about to illuminate some fatal mistake in mine. All I saw, though, was clear evidence that Joel was a better craftsman. The paint—a lavish royal blue hull with a white deck—was beautiful, the surfaces smooth and gracefully joined. The deck was nice and flat; no V-8 tumor bloated it. I also noted how skillfully Joel had orchestrated his tight one-car garage as a workshop. There was an eye-level shelf with hutches for drill, saw, router, and other tools. Next to it was a wheeled bin for wood scraps. Whenever he needed his semi-portable table saw during construction he would lay a plywood lid on the bin, set the saw on it, and roll it out to the driveway—on days it wasn't raining— where the confines of the garage wouldn't be an impediment to maneuvering wood around the saw. The workspace exhibited a quality of organization that I hadn't approached, and it was reflected in the boat's workmanship.

"If we ever go out and launch our boats together, we can rename yours for the occasion," I told him. "*Not Nearly So Far From Perfect.*"

There were possibly one or two small details in which *Far From Perfect* trumped *Not Nearly So.* Joel was having trouble fitting the exterior stem, so he just gave up, instead wrapping the bow with several layers of fiberglass cloth to survive the inevitable bumps with beach. Functionally it would be just fine, but the heavy oaken outline of *Far From Perfect*'s bow gave her an additional cut of authority, like the set of an admiral's jaw. Joel's decision had been a practical compromise. "I wanted her to look good, but I also wanted to go sailing by the end of summer."

It seemed like a reasonable trade to me, particularly since it was long past summer and I was not sailing.

I felt privately embarrassed by the beauty contest that was playing out in my head, and not just because I was losing it. What was the point of comparing our efforts? We weren't building these boats to sell, so the only competition was one we imagined. Such a thing can be destructive, battering down self-esteem to the point of paralysis. I've had writing students who quit trying and dropped out because they thought their classmates' work was on a plane unattainably far above theirs. And yet, there must be a biological reason that we *Homo sapiens* are relentlessly competitive, even where it can't possibly have anything to do with mating.

Could it be that competition is how our species makes progress—as simple as that?

As I surveyed the details of Joel's boat, I realized that his mind worked differently from mine. He anticipated problems *before* they could actually occur, and devised preventive solutions. For example, he visualized *Quality Time* capsizing and lying on her side in the water. If she were then being hammered by wind waves—altogether likely, since it would have been big wind that caused the blowdown—the commotion could cause the mast to pull free from its step. On small boats like ours, nothing but gravity normally holds the mast in place. Righting the boat, bailing it out, and then re-stepping the mast complete with wet sail, all this in a howling gale, would be impossible for a solo sailor. He'd have to cut the lines, abandon his mast and sail, and row to shore. Any witnesses standing around would have great fun, at Joel's expense, contrasting his boat's name with the fiasco they were observing. To avert all these unhappy events, he simply installed a two-dollar stainless steel pad eye on the deck, where he could lash the mast to it with a few inches of clothesline-size rope. It was the cheapest, simplest insurance I could imagine. Only I didn't imagine the problem until I saw his solution.

He has an engineer's mind, which he uses as a technical designer for Boeing. He designs the tubes, fittings, and brackets involved in jetliner fuel delivery systems, which struck me as a fairly critical job. I'd be a little worried about my next flight if his boat had looked carelessly built. My mind doesn't readily function like his, but I believe this way of thinking through problems can be learned. We liberal-arts types aren't fated to muddle helplessly through life, ignorant of physics and plumbing and electricity, unless we choose to. It's a function of patience more than a matter of aptitude: taking the time to think through a problem, consider all the directions events might take, and fabricate insurance or a rational response.

When I got home, I went out to look over *Far From Perfect*, hoping maybe to find a few extra merits somewhere, something to help justify all the time I'd lavished on her in contrast to Joel's blitz. Instead, my thinking drifted toward a potential source of future trouble that had been vaguely gnawing at me for weeks: the half-oval brass rub strips I'd screwed to the bottom of the stem and keel to help absorb impacts. Somewhere long ago I had read that when building anything that's supposed to be waterproof, you'd better train yourself to "think like water." Well, if I were water, I might just slither around those screw heads, capillary myself up into the wood, and rot it from the inside out. What fun! Thinking now like water's determined enemy, I grabbed a tube of marine caulk and built a little waterproof anthill around each screw head. It took ten minutes, and although the boat might look a little messier for it beneath the waterline, I felt a lot better.

I had been delaying actually implanting the centerboard for a good reason: I didn't want the added heft of that hunk of lead in the boat's belly during all the times we were having to flip her over. And also because of procrastination: I wasn't confident that I had drilled all the holes accurately enough that the centerboard would pivot inside the slender sandwich of its trunk, as it should. If the hole alignment proved to be off by even a couple of degrees, the centerboard would bind, or even be impossible to install. And I didn't actually know how to install it, since the pivot shaft, a big 2½-inch stainless steel bolt, was to go into a secluded cranny of the boat, hard to reach and impossible to see for the sake of alignment. I couldn't remember any other step that had depended as much on blind luck as this one.

It was a cold, gloomy, stormy January Sunday, and we were stuck indoors all day. At breakfast I asked Patty if she would help with the job.

"There's a good chance it won't work," I warned her. "But I've spent a couple of days thinking up a contingency plan, and I sort of have one. It would be a colossal amount of extra work, but at least I have an idea."

I knew exactly what she was going to say next, and she didn't disappoint me.

"If you *expect* the first try to fail, it will. Why don't you try expecting success?"

"I'm not being pessimistic, I'm being realistic. And by having a backup plan, I won't be completely demoralized if the first try fails. Unhappy, but not devastated."

We've had versions of this debate hundreds of times in our thirty-six years of marriage, usually with a reasonable degree of tolerance for each other. Her worldview hasn't been shaped by a life innocent of disappointment and even tragedy—entirely the opposite, in fact. Her father died in an airplane crash when she was sixteen, and barely two years later her fiancé was killed aboard a Navy ship in the infamous Israeli attack on the USS *Liberty*. And then there were my drinking years, when she had little cause for optimism about our future together. But she has always tried to face trouble with a positive attitude, and maintain a fierce belief in the power of faith to shape events.

She can argue persuasively that it does. In the shattering aftermath of her father's death, she was able to do a lot to hold the family together. And in the last year, she's remained unshakable in her wild belief that I can actually build this sailboat even when the prospects have looked thoroughly bleak to me. Unquestionably, that conviction has exerted a tangible force by helping me slog through the cycles of discouragement. Still, if I had been inclined to argue at the breakfast table, I would have asked her to explain to me in raw physics how positive thinking could favorably shift the alignment of holes and bolts. Since I needed her help, I didn't.

The boat was upside down on a cluster of four worktables, whose arrangement created a tunnel for me to crawl underneath.

Patty climbed a stepladder and guided the centerboard into its slot, positioning its now-invisible hole about where it should line up with the holes in the trunk. Of course it didn't. For an hour we experimented with measurements, cardboard templates, pencil marks on masking tape, wrenching the heavy centerboard in and out, and, yes, forced positive thinking—everything except what we really needed, which was X-ray vision. Until you've tried to build a boat or a clock or a fax machine, it's hard to fully appreciate what mass production has done for humanity.

For Patty, this was physically difficult and painful work. She is petite, sensitive to cold, and lately has been cursed by the arrival of arthritis in her hands. Her ten-hour weekday shifts as an oncology nurse in a busy outpatient clinic drain her energy through the week, and she needs weekends to recuperate. I had gotten peeved at her a couple of times when she'd seemed reluctant to help me with some small operation on the boat. What I really wanted was for her to begin sharing my passion for boatbuilding, to pass happy hours in the garage with me planing and sanding. But that was unrealistic and unfair; she didn't have the tolerance for physical discomfort or any compelling interest in the process. The role she wanted aligned with her weekday profession as a caregiver: providing philosophical perspective and emotional first aid. And she was unerringly good at that. This morning, though, she understood what a critical operation we were facing, and that I needed someone with more patience and commitment than I could ask from a neighbor. She wasn't complaining.

I had wormed the bolt about two-thirds of the way through, which meant it had found its way through one side of the trunk and the centerboard itself, but it hadn't located the essential hole on the trunk's opposite side. My fear was that it wouldn't find this hole because the hole was in Belgium or someplace equally far from where it was supposed to be. I had run out of ideas. "The contingency plan is going to take about three days," I groaned. "First, we plug and glass and paint over the existing holes—"

"Have you tried *everything*?" she interrupted. "Have you really thought through the problem?" I groaned again but took the question seriously because it was an appropriate one—what I'd learned about boatbuilding had convinced me that many more errors are mental than physical. In reality, the bolt was probably no more than $\frac{1}{32}$ of an inch from finding its hole. And if that was true, then maybe we could use the centerboard itself as a giant lever to move it.

I had Patty swing the centerboard up vertically—if the boat were in the water it would then have been pointing straight down—and pull it slightly toward her. With a series of pushes, pulls, and twists, we could next try pointing the bolt in four different directions and see if any one of them discovered the hole. But we didn't even need four tries—the first was the right guess. The bolt threaded itself into the final hole and I coaxed it on through with a few dozen flicks of a ratchet wrench.

Patty rotated the centerboard into its plywood nest. It grated a little, a tight fit. We wouldn't know for sure whether the alignment was good enough until we got the boat in the water and actually tried to drop the board to counter the wind. Nor would we know if the neoprene washers were snug enough around the bolt to keep water from dribbling into the boat, my enduring worry. But for the moment I was enormously relieved. Aside from a terrific cramp along the entire length of my body from pretzeling under the boat for ninety minutes, the operation went as well as it possibly could have. And it did so without the benefit of any advance optimism on my part.

But a day later, as I was outlining the operation in my builder's log and reflecting on how we did it, I suddenly realized how my cloud of negativity almost scuttled everything and triggered the dire Plan B. My exaggerated imagining that the hole was in Belgium or someplace equally far was about to block the idea for the next, and ultimately successful, strategy. Only by assuming the most *optimistic* case—that the target was no more than $\frac{1}{32}$ of an inch away—did the next action become viable.

Maureen Dowd, a columnist for *The New York Times* who has honed cynicism into high art, once wrote that "Perpetual optimism is annoying. It is a sign that you are not paying attention." That's irrefutably true, but perpetual pessimism is worse than annoying—it's automatically self-defeating. I've always believed this, and have tried to chart a realistic course between the two extremes. Aim for success, but be prepared for failure. Seems entirely reasonable. But what Patty and the centerboard appeared to have shown me was that the preparations for failure can leak into the wrong compartment of the mind, the creative gearworks, and cause everything there to seize up. Learning to avoid that would take some practice, but maybe I'd just begun.

CHAPTER 15

MIND-BENDER

A MAINE SAILOR NAMED Roger S. Duncan set out an idea that had me thinking. "People who build wooden boats have unique skills," he wrote in a book about the creation of *Dorothy Elizabeth*, a twenty-eight-foot schooner he commissioned in 1996. "Almost nothing is square or level about a boat. One needs a flexibility of mind as great as the variety of three-dimensional curves and bevels. . . ."

Flexible minds are underappreciated in these times—under attack, even—and I'll return to this broad issue in a few moments. My problem du jour on the Zephyr, though, demanded elastic thinking to figure out how to shape and implant the skeg. This is a five-foot-long fin that serves to help the boat track straight and also shields the more fragile rudder from scrapes on rock and beach. I'd already cut out the rough wedge shape of the skeg from a ¾-inch white oak board, but then I faced the problem of trimming and mating it to the curving centerline of the hull.

There are expensive template tools that precisely trace curves like this, but Peter Gron had inspired me to try thinking outside the toolbox. He showed me how he'd made dozens of improvised plywood clamps for about a Canadian buck apiece. They were stunning in their sheer simplicity, and the way Peter came up with them was to look hard at the problem itself instead of surveying the existing options—the different types of commercial clamps. At issue was how to squeeze the sheer clamp, a twenty-four-foot-long wooden strip, tightly against the hull while its glue cured. Forty-eight C-clamps at five bucks apiece would have done nicely. Instead, the skinflint Peter cut out a pile of scrap plywood brackets in the shape of square-cornered horseshoes, and made a doorstop-like wedge to accompany each one. He then slipped the horseshoes over the sheer and "tightened" them with the wooden wedges. It was medieval technology, but it was economical and perfectly adequate for the job—and elegant in how it so precisely addressed the problem.

I made a run to Home Depot with no plan except to wander the aisles and see what, if anything, occurred to me. I paused in the millwork department, mentally bending a piece of thin pine molding to match the keel line, then cobbling together a complicated template with a truss of dowels and braces. It would have looked like a model for a bridge—impressive in its refinement, but needlessly complicated for the job at hand. I was trying to think along the lines of Occam's Razor: the simplest solution to a problem is likely to be the best. Slogging toward the tool department, I passed a bin of rough, near-throwaway cedar boards that just happened to measure five feet long. That was it! I bought two of them for $1.29 apiece.

My idea was to bandsaw the curve on one of them as well as I could by eye, refine it by trial, error, and sandpaper, then use it as a template to lay out the curve on the much harder white oak skeg. Since cedar is soft and the scrap pieces were thin, they would be easy to shape. Having a second one on hand would serve as cheap insurance against messing up the first.

It almost worked. After a couple of hours I saw that it wasn't quite possible to fit the skeg template precisely to the curve of the keel. Every time I erased the last $\frac{1}{16}$-inch gap in one place, it created a new one somewhere down the line. In light of my history, a $\frac{1}{16}$-inch gap wasn't bad. I declared the job done and sawed the skeg to the template's arc. Then I chiseled out a little trough in the skeg's new curve so it would mate more gracefully with the shallow V of the hull shape, lathered it generously with glop, and planted it vertically on the hull with a spirit level.

It was essential that the skeg grip the hull mightily. Along with the stem, it's the part of the boat most likely to suffer abuse. In effect, these are the boat's bumpers. I ran two layers of glass cloth along the bottom of the hull and up the sides of the skeg, and over the course of two days saturated the whole works with five coats of epoxy. Since the skeg was vertical, the glop ran and sagged with gravity, creating a congealed mess that cost hours of sanding. But the dusty work was better than going out in a flimsy boat.

I'd decided some time ago to leave the underwater area of the hull with a Grade C finish—who's to be offended, beyond salmon and mussels?—but after pondering Peter's bronzed urn of a hull, I was suffering pangs of guilt and inferiority. It was a reprise of high school, alarmingly. My two best friends were straight-A students, which eventually shamed me into ratcheting up my average, tediously and resentfully, to a B-minus.

Unfortunately, this minor eruption of quality-control conscience arrived at the same time as a frigid early-winter storm, which dumped four inches of snow on us and sent the thermometer skidding to twenty degrees. Nobody would even notice this in Chicago or London, but it paralyzed Seattle. The school around the corner closed for three days, and nobody on our street even tried to leave for work. I threw open the garage door for ventilation—essential even though it was well below freezing—and mounted a fresh attack on the rough hull and skeg with the orbital sander. More guilt: the tool poured a profane racket into the street, where a sabbath-like serenity had descended with the snow. It was hard work, rendered harder by the cold. After the first two hours my fingers were almost immobile from the chill, my back ached from leaning over the hull, and my eyes had acquired a crust of grit from the airborne epoxy dust—and it was time to brush on another layer of glop so I could do the same thing again tomorrow.

After five days of this I had a sturdy skeg and a Grade B hull, and I had arrived at a pivotal moment in the gestation of *Far From Perfect*: she was ready to paint.

The exercise with the skeg, in concert with events in the news, has kept me thinking about the virtues of the flexible mind.

This is no small matter. It's at the core of survival—definitely at the level of the individual and the tribe, and maybe in the macrocosm of civilization itself.

I've been reading the works of a thoughtfully analytical writer named Laurence Gonzalez who specializes, of all things, in outdoor-adventure disaster. In his book *Deep Survival: Who Lives, Who Dies, and Why*, Gonzalez analyzed dozens of accounts of mountain climbing, river rafting, and backcountry skiing mishaps, many of them with tragic endings. Gonzalez's conclusion, distilled to its basic principle, is this: The people who get into trouble out there are the ones who cling tenaciously to their original plan or to an idealized model of their environment even as conditions around them deteriorate. An example would be a mountaineer who presses on for the summit instead of turning around when ominous storm clouds begin closing in. Instead of objectively assessing the real world of the present, he's stuck in the twelve-hour-old model of the weather forecast, which had predicted more agreeable conditions. He's in denial. He's trying to twist reality to his expectations, rather than revising those expectations. If you could stop him and explain his behavior in just those terms, he might see it as the irrational act it is. Or he might not, because that obsolete forecast has woven itself into his emotional craving for the summit, and he's locked in. This inflexibility may kill him. The survivors, Gonzalez says, are those who are willing to let go of a plan that's decreasingly likely to work and smartly consider a new constellation of possibilities. He proclaims outright, "Rigid people are dangerous people." And he quotes the Zen master Shunryu Suzuki on the wisdom of remaining open and teachable: "In the beginner's mind there are many possibilities. In the expert's mind there are few."

In the decade that I've been paddling, I've closely monitored fatal sea kayaking accidents—there are generally two or three every year in North America—and I've noticed that most of the victims separate into two categories. They're either rank beginners who blunder into a situation they don't understand, or they're top-drawer experts who assume they can handle anything. The safest paddlers are those of us in the vast middle who have a reasonable store of knowledge and skills, coupled with a humbling fear of weather and the sea. I consciously work to maintain a likeness of that beginner's mind, remaining aware that the marine environment holds a fathomless range of options for disposing of a forty-pound boat and its ridiculous occupant. (I was once chased by a five-hundred-pound sea lion, as if to confirm the ludicrous lengths to which ol' Neptune will go.)

The flexible mind constantly evaluates the changing environment and charts the most appropriate response. And connects a feedback loop. When an action fails to work, don't just repeat it—change it. Foolish consistency is indeed the hobgoblin of little minds, but also something much worse: it has rained misery on entire nations and cultures. The endless cycle of revenge and retribution between Israel and the Palestinians is one depressing example; the United States's dogmatic approach to a widening circle of adversaries—Iraq, Iran, North Korea—is another, possibly even more ominous. Around the opening of the twenty-first century, dogmatism somehow acquired an upright standing, as if it were the structural fiber of morality. It isn't, unless you think fondly of the Inquisition.

It seems to me that relations between nations and religions would be more productive if we negotiated with each other like Gonzalez suggests we climb mountains: deal with what actually *is*, not with what we think *ought* to be.

As I think back over the building of *Far From Perfect* I realize that lesson has been there at every turn, and as the building progressed I got better at recognizing it. When my beautiful $99 cedar centerboard cracked after a mere tip-over on the garage floor, I was at least flexible enough not to keep trying to force it to work when the nature of the material was arguing to the contrary. The challenge now is to expand that precept into the larger sphere of life. For example, I've been clinging to an obsolete model in my magazine writing, resenting a certain well-known magazine for not wanting any more of the relatively long, exploratory travel pieces I used to write for them. But none of my carping and whining has altered the magazine's new direction, nor is it likely to. How many of us hold on desperately to jobs that aren't working for us any more, or to careers that are becoming obsolete, unfulfilling, or meaningless? Instead of changing, we retreat into the warm cocoon of denial and hold on, because change is frightening: there's no road map, no guarantee of success.

I may have drifted far away from what Roger Duncan meant by "flexibility of mind." But that requirement for creative but practical thinking may be the deepest beauty of all imbedded in a boat, because the builder gets endless practice in figuring things out, discarding dogmas, adjusting to new realities. This is how civilizations, as well as individuals, make progress.

Sam Devlin's Zephyr is an undeniably simple design, and yet there was almost nothing about it that was proving to be simple for a virgin boatbuilder. The next issue was paint. I gathered half a dozen book chapters, magazine articles, and marine paint manufacturers' pamphlets on how to paint a boat, and all I gleaned from them was two words: it depends.

On what the boat is made of, how it's going to be stored, how it's going to be used, what latitude and climate it's going to reside in, what kind of primer (if any) you apply, what kind of paint you choose (there are at least a dozen different formulations of marine paint) what kind of brush (or spray) you use, and the alignment of Mars's two moons, Deimos and Phobos, at the moment you pop the can of paint. OK, I made that last one up, but there are so many variables, and so many different opinions, that astrology might as well be stirred into the can.

I had made one big decision: red. Interlux, one of the major marine paint companies, makes a dark, bloody hue called "Bounty" that looks so deep and rich that it could swallow up your reflection and it would free-fall into eternity. I couldn't resist, despite an entire page of dire Devlin warnings about the perils of painting boats *any* dark color. Dark paint shows off surface imperfections, with which my boat was legion. It can even absorb so much heat in the sun that the epoxy underneath begins to soften, which could result in a suddenly flexible boat.

But this was one choice I had made by emotion: I wanted a red sailboat.

With the boat turned over, I brushed on a test patch of about ten square feet on the B-minus port bottom and a couple more square feet on the B-plus starboard side. It looked stunning. I left it for the night, and the next morning I was up at five to see how it had dried. Both patches looked awful. They were speckled with dust, streaked with bristle marks, uneven, splotchy, runny, and broadcasting glorious surface imperfections to all the world.

I burrowed into my pile of references to learn how much of this I could fix. Quite a lot, it turned out. One obvious issue was that my garage by this time had more than a year's worth of accumulated boat dust on the floor, and every footstep in the vicinity was launching some of it into the air, poised to waft into the wet paint. An article by Aimé Fraser in *WoodenBoat* magazine advised me to apply thinner coats. "Most bad paint jobs are caused in one way or another by trying to put on too much too fast," he wrote, which is the sort of dog-simple instruction I could absorb. Fraser also recommended throwaway foam instead of expensive bristle brushes, which seemed like a dubious proposition. But I was taking flexible-mind practice, so I was willing to try it.

I borrowed a friend's Shop-Vac, spent a long afternoon cleaning the garage and then the bare hull itself, then went out to buy expensive marine paint thinner and a bagful of sixty-five-cent foam brushes. It took about two hours to apply a thin coat to the entire hull, and it was pleasurable work. Painting was a morale-booster: no other step in the building process had made such a dramatic turn in the boat's appearance so quickly. And Fraser was right about the foam; it laid down a smoother coat than the brush and didn't leave a wake of orphaned bristles.

There was one immediate problem. Long months earlier, when I had cut out pieces of fiberglass cloth for sheathing the hull's exterior, I had grabbed an old green permanent marker and scribbled an identifying label on each piece: PORT 2, STARBD 3 and so on. These directions were now screaming brightly through the paint. I wondered how many coats it would take to cover them up.

Four more mornings in a row I lightly sanded the previous day's work, thoroughly cleaned the hull with a tack cloth, and applied another coat. STARBD 3 was remarkably tenacious; it didn't give up until the fifth round. I craved for this to be the final coat, but it didn't look great. There were runs and drips and wavy patches that needed to be sanded, and then what— still another coat? Where would it end? Devlin's final words in his "Painting" chapter only informed me that ". . . you need a lot of patience, and a similar amount of luck." Thanks, friend.

At this point I had regressed to a five-yard boat, and however brilliant and glorious the color, my impatient or unlucky paint job had degraded my hard-won Grade B hull to a mousy C or worse. I couldn't find any article titled "Salvaging a Crummy Paint Job," so I seemed to be on my own. Flexibility was urgently needed.

Thirty years ago Patty and I owned a beloved old Peugeot whose red paint had oxidized severely in the Arizona sun. We couldn't afford then to have it repainted, so I took a can of polishing compound—a last resort, unaccompanied by much hope—and spent a hot afternoon in the carport wiping and rubbing. It worked far better than expected, restoring the paint to near-showroom luster. On the slim promise of that experience, I developed a plan for rescuing the boat paint: Clean up the errors with two or three rounds of increasingly fine sandpaper, then go over the entire hull with grade oooo steel wool (so fine it feels almost velvety), then polishing compound, and finally automotive wax.

Before committing to all this, I tried it on a dinner plate-sized section of the bottom. To my utter amazement, it worked. The worst of the scratches, streaks, and runs disappeared. The surface assumed a soft sheen, breaking up reflected light into a satiny glow instead of mirrored images. It's what you want for a wooden boat, actually—a surface that looks carefully though imperfectly handcrafted instead of one that tries to imitate factory production.

It took three full afternoons to commit this four-step procedure on the entire hull. It was seriously fatiguing work, and I had no idea whether it was valid boat painting—nothing in my pile of references described anything remotely like what I was doing. Maybe it would all dissolve three minutes after *Far From Perfect* hit salt water. At the moment, though, it looked damned good.

I think that in building a boat, you have to chart an uncertain and necessarily wobbly path between asking advice and following directions on one hand, and figuring things out for yourself on the other. If you simply want to follow directions, you should build a kit. Nothing wrong with that, except humanity would never make any progress if we built only kits.

At the other extreme is the trust-thyself-above-all commandment of Emerson: "A man should learn to detect and watch that gleam of light which flashes across his mind from within, more than the lustre of the firmament of bards and sages." However noble and eloquent that sounds, it exudes the ominous whiff of dogma. A flexible mind dances between the external chorus of other people's experience, and the internal siren of invention or conviction. In the end, it boils down to this, which to me has always seemed like a more than adequate philosophy of life: whatever works is good.

Chapter 16

EBB TIDE

"She's looking great. But I don't see your deck brace in the photos. Did you take it out for better access?"

It's an e-mail from Joel Bergen. I'm staring at the screen, trying to digest what he means, and suddenly I feel the hot dagger pangs of alarm, physically, right in my gut. Like I've boarded a flight for Tucson, only the plane is taxiing to the runway and the attendant has just announced our flying time to: Miami. Deck brace? I think I remember seeing the piece he's referring to on the Zephyr he built—a richly varnished slab of okoume plywood underneath the forward rail of the coaming. I had assumed it was cosmetic. His use of the term "brace" seems to imply something more critical.

I hurry out to the garage to consult Devlin's plans. There it is, or was, on the final sheet: a four-foot-long frame piece that could be made either of plywood or cedar, spanning the boat from one side of the hull to the other at the forward edge of the cockpit. You don't have to be an engineer to see that it's indeed a brace, an integral piece of the boat's structure. But I didn't see it at all, unobtrusively lurking in the plans amid a thicket of larger bulkheads and hull pieces. I should have made and installed it in November, four months back, before I locked down the deck.

Early in this adventure, my reaction would have been to take decisive action, borne on wings of panic. Grab pencil, saw, and chisels, and retrofit the truant brace, whatever the cost in labor and appearance. But this isn't an emergency, it's a problem—one that I can at least contemplate for a while. It's not procrastination if you're using time to legitimately think through a problem and avoid compounding a mistake. I haven't been very good at making this distinction, historically—I either bluster ahead with the first fix that pops into my head, or shunt the problem to a cold burner forever. *Far From Perfect* actually may be teaching me a new way of working. I think the reason is that I have so much invested in her at this point that I'm fiercely wary of doing anything dumb.

At the same time, I'm deeply worried that I've already done something dumb.

Far From Perfect's story to this point has been a tidal cycle of emotional highs and lows, peaks of pleasure and optimism followed by troughs of fatigue and discouragement. What's happening now is a convergence of lows, some of them outside the scope of the boat. My father is still alive, against all his caregivers' expectations, but the last discernible quality has drained out of his life. I've made five trips to El Paso to try to solve problems and offer some comfort, but it feels like we are in a confined space of emotion that we are still unable to navigate. At home I'm fixating on *Far From Perfect*'s flaws, and no self-administered pep talk or reasoning seems to make it go away. I don't have the craftsmanship to make everything happen as it should—corners mitered with furniture-like precision, epoxy skin as smooth as glass. It's eerily reminiscent of where I was twenty years ago when I quit the piano: I now know enough about boatbuilding to visualize exactly what I want, but I don't have the chops to make it happen. I'm surprised that such a persistent malaise has settled in now, so close to the end. I don't like my emotions being so deeply tied into the boat with a life of their own that I can't control.

A few days ago I actually was about to board a flight to Tucson when I bumped into Ken Slade, another Boeing engineer I know in Seattle. It's a mixed blessing to build a boat in a town crawling with aircraft designers: they cheerfully volunteer their expertise, much of which translates seamlessly from aircraft to watercraft, but they're in the habit of fishing for potential problems everywhere in the pond.

Ken studied photos of my boat-in-progress while we waited for our flight, and then started questioning me about various points of structure. I proudly explained all my beefy bracing under the mast, where the wind force will translate into horsepower to propel the boat. He seemed satisfied, if not impressed. His eyes roamed to the boat's stern. "What do you have at the corners where the transom meets the sides of the hull?" he asked.

"Epoxy fillets and glass."

"How big are the fillets?"

"A little less than an inch radius." I demonstrated with my thumb. "Why?"

"Those joints are where all the loads from the rudder end up."

"I made them pretty much according to Devlin's plan."

"I'd be glad to come over and look at them for you."

"You can't get at them. They're underneath the deck and behind a big block of flotation foam."

"I'd be a little worried about them," he concluded, helpfully.

I'd be a little happier if he had praised my muscle-bound mast step or fiberglassed centerboard trunk or the double layer of plywood reinforcing the side decks, but I guess that isn't what they do at Boeing. Nor, for obvious reasons, do they test aircraft by the empirical method: fly 'em until something literally falls apart, then redesign the failed piece a little stronger. Ken explained that they employ ground testing that simulates the stresses of twenty-five years of flying, bending a wing, for example, until it breaks. Lacking such an engineering department, my possibly half-cocked plan is to sail *Far From Perfect* in winds that gradually progress up the scale, hoping that any part that's about to croak will issue a warning groan or screech enough in advance that I can do something about it—or if it doesn't, praying that its failure will be merely embarrassing rather than catastrophic. This plan, of course, will depend on predictable and cooperative weather, an unusual condition in nature.

Here is my functional worry list:

- The rudder, which swivels off the transom on two pairs of stainless-steel widgets called pintles and gudgeons. I don't know if the gudgeons are screwed securely enough to the transom or if the working end of the rudder will wobble and flutter or even torque itself loose because there's no attachment point down low. I tried twice to install a third gudgeon, but it proved impossible to align with the other two.

- The gooseneck, another specialized steel gadget that allows the boom to rotate around the mast in both the vertical and horizontal planes. I paid $22.88 for one designed for "small boats," which decidedly describes the Zephyr, but it seems awfully petite and delicate to digest the stress of an angry ten-foot boom slamming through the wind.
- The axle for the centerboard, which lurks below the waterline in the centerboard trunk. If it leaks, it's going to be a colossal undertaking to fix it. And if the centerboard binds in either its up or down position, I'll be in a boat that can't be fully controlled under sail or can't get to shore without grounding the board.
- The transom-to-side joints, thanks to Ken Slade's scrutiny.
- The nonexistent deck brace, thanks to Joel Bergen's review.

It's a March afternoon, uncharacteristically sunny and warm enough for some quality time working on the boat, but after a few token probes with my fingers under the deck to test the feasibility of implanting a deck brace—conclusion: not easy—I go inside. Instead of making a boat, I make a New Mexican enchilada sauce for dinner. Butter, flour, chicken stock, powdered Chimayó and pasilla chile, cumin, honey. The pungent earthiness is an aromatic balm. I've been looking forward more and more to the hour I spend every weekday making dinner for Patty as a kind of organic tranquilizer to smooth over the emotional serrations left by the afternoon's boat work. I feel completely competent in the kitchen; I don't often make mistakes and don't agonize over them when I do. My cooking, an avocation into which I long ago settled into a zone of comfort, is now giving the relief from boatbuilding that boatbuilding was supposed to give from writing.

While the enchilada sauce is simmering, I write Peter Gron a note:

> Have you had to fight through cycles of discouragement? Every evening after I finish work I seem to limp into the house feeling crappy because of another mistake or uncertainty about the meaning and value of this whole exercise. I don't know where this is coming from, since I thought I came to terms with a fairly high ambient level of imperfection a long time ago.

He replies early the next morning:

> I think it has to do, partly, with grieving. No, really! This (as you near completion) is where you finally, really, come to grips with the level of quality that you've achieved. You may be grieving the opportunity to make it better.

I had sent the same note to Joel, and he also has a thoughtful reply:

> It's easy to get discouraged when we make mistakes. None of us are professional boatbuilders. We've never taken on a project anywhere near this magnitude. We don't know what we're doing from the outset, and we frequently get conflicting advice. But because we're amateurs it's OK if we make mistakes. My boat has plenty. The bow is about three inches to port, giving *Quality Time* a banana shape. My rudder is off

center despite my doing everything I could possibly think of to center it accurately. I could go on and on, but you know what? None of this bothers me. The imperfections are just reminders of the new skills I've learned and how I've grown. And finally, when I put my boat in the water and climb on board, all my worries and problems fade away.

I chew on Peter's and Joel's words over the next several days of work. I think Peter is right about the grief. I'm astonished to learn that Joel's boat curls like a banana on its side—I never noticed, which might be prima facie evidence that such cosmetic defects really *don't* matter. I'm annoyed with myself for struggling, apparently, with a resurgence of the perfectionist demon. I thought I'd killed it a year ago.

But perfectionism is a complex beast, and not something you can easily broom away with go-easy-on-yourself aphorisms or even hard reasoning. In the broad sweep of human affairs, perfectionism is not a bad thing. Voltaire famously said, "The best is the enemy of the good," but the observation is just as valid if we whirl it around: The good is the enemy of the best. In many cases, pushing for perfection is clearly the right thing to do. It can even be a moral imperative. Where would we be in air travel if Boeing weren't continually striving to make the perfectly safe airliner? Fifty years ago flying was vastly more hazardous than it is today. But consider Brahms, the classic self-torturing perfectionist. He relentlessly burned scores that didn't meet his own standards, and once told a protégé (whose music we have easily forgotten) that "you seem to me too easily satisfied. . . . I never cool down over a work, once begun, until it's perfected, unassailable." Brahms's perfect music has enriched humanity beyond measure, but my reading of his life is that it also extracted an enormous price in the composer's personal misery. He sought perfection in love and friendship, but because human behavior, unlike his musical creations, was beyond his control, he failed again and again. He lived a lonely and anguished life.

We seem to be confronting a perfect dilemma. For the individual, striving for perfection, or even objective excellence, is often personally destructive. But for the sake of humanity, it's essential. Without this drive, we don't enrich the quality of life on earth.

The answer must be to find a balance, but I'm stymied. I've become too emotionally entangled in the boat, and it's blackening my mood almost every day because the quality isn't there. I want to pull back, disengage my emotions and self-esteem from the project, but I don't know how. The entanglement of boat and mind—this would not surprise Steinbeck or E. B. White— has assumed a life of its own that isn't under control.

Relief, at least temporary, appears in the form of a Mort Gerberg cartoon, of all things. I'm avoiding work on the boat one afternoon by reading *The New Yorker*, and here's this bored-looking cubicle drudge talking to another: "I say, if at first you don't succeed, redefine success." That might be the solution. Maybe *Far From Perfect* is just a rehearsal, a way station on the road to building a real boat. Would that be so bad?

There's enough daylight and initiative left today for one of my little jobs: another coat of varnish on the mast. First, I have to sand off the blob-like dribbles from the preceding coat that accumulated because I let the mast dry lying horizontally instead of vertically. After brushing on a better, but still imperfect, coat, I prop it up outside against the garage eaves, taking care to tape a scrap of wax paper where it makes contact. And I feel like I've arrived at a crossroads. It's time to sprint to the end—to just finish the boat. To quit grieving, quit worrying, quit yearning for an alternate universe where amateurs enjoy an infinite span of time to blossom with professional skills. The deck is just going to have to brace itself. The varnish will have to do for now; it can be improved later—if it seems worth the effort.

This is the thought that lifts me over the wall: the one thing that's more irrational than building your own boat is becoming so obsessive that you fail at building it.

I can't remember the last time I followed the troubleshooting instructions that came with a product and they actually worked, promptly and perfectly. If the instructions actually address the problem at hand, a rare enough occurrence, then the recommended solution is either ambiguous, incomprehensible, or impossible.

I'm pondering the oak veneer Patty helped me glue to the deck last night, and it's heartbreaking. On the forward deck erupt eight or ten veneer tumors, swollen ovoid bumps where stowaway air bubbles slipped underneath and we didn't see them in the crummy night lighting. I can't ignore them because the forward deck already has that master bulge from being forced down onto bulkheads that weren't shaped right, and the effect of all these additional baby bulges is like Quasimodo breaking out in measles—surely the last thing the poor schmuck needs. I've got to get rid of them, and the obvious solution, ripping up seventy-five bucks' worth of veneer fastened down with contact cement, is not appealing.

A miniature booklet that came from Virginia with the veneer, however, suggests: "Deflate the air bubbles by slitting them in the direction of the grain and pressing toward the slit. In a circular motion, work around the bubbled area with a warm, dry iron until the blisters are firmly set."

It adds that one should inspect for bubbles and commence treatment within two hours after laying down the veneer. It's now been ten. The chance that this is going to work seems vanishingly small. But I don't have a Plan B, so I fetch the iron from the laundry room.

I circle all the malignancies with a pencil, slit them, fire up the iron, and attack the smallest one, taking care to place a kitchen towel between the iron and wood so I don't scorch it. After working the iron around in the prescribed circular motion, I leave its point resting over the bubble for a few seconds to hopefully reactivate the contact cement underneath. I remove the iron, and I'm astonished: the bubble has vanished. Unfortunately, there's also the amber outline of a Presto steam iron where I last parked it. But the veneer isn't scorched, just slightly discolored, and a few passes with sandpaper erase the problem. I attack the rest of the bumps, following the instructions *exactly*—it takes conscious effort to avoid introducing personal innovations like parking the iron—and in twenty minutes the deck is in remission. No tumors (except for Big Mama), no visible slits, no iron-shaped discolorations. A little touch-up sanding of the seams and edges, and the deck will be ready for its clear protective layer of glass and glop.

At this not-quite-final stage, *Far From Perfect* looks superficially impressive. The richly grained white oak veneer, which I chose to match the solid oak of the stem and tiller, provides a beautiful visual counterpoint to the hull's deep bing-cherry paint. It would have been less trouble, and much less expensive, just to paint the deck a contrasting white, as Joel did with his Zephyr, but I wanted to broadcast some unmistakable evidence that this is a *wooden* boat. Of course my effort won't hold up under philosophical attack: the veneer is a costume, not representative of the plywood underneath and playing no part in the structure of the boat. In a philosophically and aesthetically perfect world, natural materials would always express themselves honestly, never needing dress or decoration. But the world isn't perfect, and I'm far from the accomplished level of boatbuilding at which I could indulge the luxury of philosophical integrity. I still have to cover some things up.

I dress the deck in fiberglass cloth and brush a coat of epoxy glop over it. As always, the cloth turns transparent and invisible, and the glop forms a glistening though wavy and dimpled shell over it. My epoxy technique doesn't seem to be improving. It's good enough for some deceptively pretty photos, though, so I shoot a few and e-mail them to select friends.

The next step is to make and install the coaming, the three-inch-high frame around the cockpit that will double as backrest and last-ditch levee to keep the water out when the boat heels. It would be an easy job except that the cockpit isn't a pure rectangle—its sides curve in a concave arc to echo the contours of the deck, and when the coaming is installed its sides will cant outward a few degrees off the vertical to reflect the slope of the deck. So the ends of the cedar pieces have to mate at about ninety-four degrees instead of the right angles of a nice box, they have to join at a slight slope, and they have to be coaxed to bend in the middle: all this at once. I actually measure all these perverse angles with a protractor and pretend to cut out the pieces as precision components—spare parts for the Hubbell space telescope, I tell myself, trying to get into the mood of exacting craftsmanship—but the results are laughably inexact and I throw the first three efforts away. Then it's back to the cut-and-try method: I cut each of the four sides slightly too long, wedge them in place, squint, scratch on some vague pencil marks, and cut again. And again. After about three hours of this, I have an acceptable coaming, ready to render permanent with bronze screws and glue. I'm fatigued from the tedious fitting process, so I just eyeball the screw positions—I think I'm getting pretty good at this—and drill holes for them without bothering to measure. My line of screws looks like a herd of cats. I conduct a brief internal skirmish of conscience and decide I just can't let them go. I fill the holes and re-drill.

With the coaming in place, the boat suddenly seems substantially more real, more three-dimensional. And now I'm energized. For a couple of months I've been incubating an idea to extend the visual line of the coaming out behind the cockpit, with a pair of flying buttresses three inches high and two feet long, tapering like swoops into the aft deck. I don't know of any sailboat that has such a thing, but I'm recalling the roofline of the late '70s Ferrari 308GTB, one of the most breathtakingly beautiful cars ever designed. Making the cedar swoops takes just a few minutes with the bandsaw, and I lay them in place on the aft deck just behind the coaming. They look great, but I'm suddenly throttled by nagging doubts. Are they *appropriate*? What about Peter Gron's belief that a sailboat's innate beauty is a direct consequence of functionality? Do my flying buttresses sabotage the spiritual integrity of the boat? They have no function except to remind me of a dream car, but is that so bad?

After twenty minutes of studying the swoops from every possible angle I take them off and throw them away, and I feel a flood of instant relief. It's like I just decided to not commit a sin.

The last major step is the rigging, setting up the mast, boom, sprit pole, sail, and sail controls. All this has to be temporary, easily installed and removed, since *Far From Perfect* will reside in the garage and ride to her launch sites on a trailer—far from practical if there's a twelve-foot mast permanently planted in her deck.

The sprit rig, which dates from the late nineteenth century, offers the advantage of simplicity. A sail roughly the shape of Virginia is simply laced to the mast with slippery polyester rope (or *line*, as sailors insist it be called when in use on a boat) and its peak stretched into the sky by a light, skinny pole called the sprit. It provides a lot of sail area for a relatively short mast, which translates directly into power for the boat. Several authoritative books on American sailboat history praise it to the skies: ". . . the most efficient and practical of all small-boat sails"; "one of the handiest and most useful rigs . . ." Its one disadvantage is that it won't sail upwind as well as today's triangular rigs. But around Seattle you're as likely to find a calliope on a sailboat as a sprit rig; almost nobody I've talked to knows much about them. The local sail lofts I consulted seemed uninterested in bothering with my pipsqueak sail; the lowest bid was a breathtaking $580. (For perspective, the Zephyr's spritsail is four square feet larger than a flat king bedsheet.) I finally found a sailmaker in a tiny landlocked east Texas town who crafted a nice Dacron sail to specification for $318, including shipping. I ordered a red one; I'm thinking the distinctive color will invest a small sailboat with an extra ration of drama. The color is actually called "tanbark" because it evokes the ruddy tint of historic sails dipped in tannin derived from tree bark. When sails could only be made of cotton, the tannin solution was the sailmakers' best shot at retarding rot and mold.

I don't actually know how to set up the rig. Devlin's plan is vague on details. Joel Bergen engineered his rig with a free-range boom, which I don't understand at all. But between sifting through Googled esoterica on the sprit rig and wandering the docks at the Center for Wooden Boats, studying more conventional sloop-rigged small boats, I figure it out. The boom has to join the mast in a secure but completely flexible T-intersection; the sprit must suspend the sail from its top and angle away from the mast near the bottom with a tension-adjusting line called, no joke, a "snotter." Then I'll install a line called the mainsheet at the free end of the boom to control the sail's movements to port or starboard. Since the Zephyr is so small, there's no need for the Mr. Wizard array of sail adjustments you find on a modern cruising or racing boat. Still, it takes me a couple of three-hour afternoon sessions to drill all the requisite holes and encrust the mast and boom with their hardware, and bathe the rest of the wood in another coat of varnish to protect it from weather. There's also a problem with the hole in the deck—it's called the mast partner—into which the mast fits. For appearance's sake it needs some kind of ceremonial collar so it doesn't look like, well, a hole in the deck.

I cut a basic beveled picture frame out of four strips of oak. But the two cross-pieces won't lie flat on the deck because of its peaky centerline.

I run through a mental register of options, all of them groan-inducing: bed the frame on a pond of glop, steam-bend the strips, or attempt a hopelessly precise bevel. After thirty minutes of unconventionally hard thinking I hatch an unconventional idea. It probably won't work, but all I'm risking is mangling a couple of four-inch oak strips. I mark a couple of crosswise lines on their backs, then use the bandsaw to take slim, V-shaped sections out of them. I saw not quite all the way through the strips, so I can bend them to conform to the deck.

And it works! The picture frame embraces the hole almost elegantly, and the bend is subtle enough that it'll only be evident if some Pecksniffian weenie inspects the job. I don't think this is authorized boatbuilding technique or bandsaw employment, but it might be evidence of an embryonic "flexibility of mind," as Roger Duncan put it, beginning to limber up and twist a bit. Or it might be an amateur's expedience.

Maybe these are the same thing.

The final Sunday afternoon in March grants us an uncharacteristic blue sky, a few cumulus puffs with nothing to do, and barely a breath of breeze. Not much good for sailing, but it's perfect for low-stress testing the rig in the driveway. Patty and I wheel *Far From Perfect* out on her new trailer—a surprise gift from Dr. Doug Lee, one of the oncologists in the clinic where Patty works—and rig the sail flat on the lawn. Then together we lift the mast, boom, sprit, and sail assembly and drop it into the step.

We haven't noticed, but several neighbors have been watching all this from their windows. As a wisp of wind catches the red sail and tailors it into the curving airfoil shape it will need to sail close-hauled into the wind, swinging the boom gently to port, the street breaks out in applause.

Chapter 17

Birth Day

April 8, Easter Sunday. *Far From Perfect* is "finished," at least to the extent that we can put her in the water and learn how, or whether, she sails; and develop a punch list of things that need to be changed or improved. I make a smoked salmon omelet for breakfast, spend a little more time than usual with the Sunday paper, and finally call up the hour-by-hour weather forecast on my laptop. It looks like our best window for sailing will lie between eleven and two, when the predicted wind is southwest at eight miles an hour and the chance of rain is only 40 percent. Later promises wetter.

I'm perturbed by the midday window. I'd hoped to put the launch off till late afternoon, spend most of the day doing something fun. I'm not looking forward to the launch. I feel like I'm anticipating some medical procedure where the doctor keeps dodging questions about whether it's supposed to hurt.

These emotions are strange and disconcerting and not under control. It's not at all like I had envisioned this day eighteen months back, nothing like a triumphant christening for a micro-yacht. At least twenty friends have asked to come to the launch, and I waved each one off with whatever vague excuse I could devise for the moment. Partly it's that I just don't *feel* triumphant or deserving of a ceremony: the boat is too far from perfect. The other issue is that I'm worried about embarrassment. Today is a convergence of two things I still know too little about: boatbuilding and sailing.

At least we have a forgiving venue at hand. We'll launch at Beaver Lake, a pretty half-mile-long lake less than a mile from our house. Powerboats are prohibited, so the only traffic there is other slow-moving boats: kayaks, canoes, fishing dinghies with electric trolling motors. Patty and I have often taken friends over there to introduce them to kayaking in the safest possible environment. Oddly, I've never seen a sailboat actually sailing.

I start assembling turkey sandwiches and a tool kit for on-site modifications. Patty says she's going to wear her wetsuit. At first I think she's joking, but she's serious.

"It kind of hurts my feelings that you're expecting a capsize," I tell her.

"I'm not," she protests. "It's just for wading in to launch the boat."

I don't think I believe her. We've never seen anyone wearing a wetsuit to sail except for the Laser and Sunfish racers, who *expect* to get dunked. Somewhere under my irritation, I know she's just smart to be prepared. I'd wear my wetsuit too, but it would feel like I'm jinxing my boat.

At 10:30 a.m. we stash the sail rig in the cockpit, hook up the trailer, and trundle it to the lake. The fishermen are out in droves—a couple of them at the crowded launch site, at least a dozen on the lake. I'd like to wait till Monday for more privacy, but it's supposed to rain all day.

I back the trailer inexpertly to the edge of the lake, and we lift the mast and sail into its step. I thread the mainsheet through a miniature block and a plastic jam cleat mounted on the tiller, and she's ready to go—this is the simplest rigging of any sailboat in existence. I back the trailer another twenty feet, and we gingerly roll *Far From Perfect* off into the water. With her centerboard up she floats in six inches. I stare at the rubber washers where the centerboard axle bursts through the trunk and see no trace of Beaver Lake dribbling into my boat. Scratch one worry: if it were going to leak, this would be the place.

Patty restrains *Far From Perfect* by her bowline, like a dog on a leash, while I park the car and trailer. I'm beginning to feel slightly optimistic. No leaks, and the wind is so light that it can't possibly capsize us. I wade into the water, pants rolled above knee-high rubber boots, and climb aboard alone. I want Patty to stay on shore while I get the feel of the boat. I suddenly realize, absurdly: I've never sailed a boat with a centerboard instead of a ballasted keel. I barely know how to do this even in theory. I'll probably capsize it *without* any wind.

A feathery breeze politely abducts the sail, swings it to starboard. I paddle a couple of strokes to bring the bow around so the wind is perpendicular to the boat—a beam reach in sailing parlance, the easiest point of sail to manage. *Far From Perfect* begins to move under wind power. Slowly, no more than a casual strolling pace on land, but moving, wholly under the borrowed power of the wind. I suddenly feel a joy as deep and almost as ineffable as my earlier dread and depression.

Where's it coming from? It's not so much about accomplishment, but rather authenticity, engaging in something that is real, that obeys comprehensible laws of the universe, that is anchored thousands of years deep in human culture. The shape of the sail, the grain of the wooden form around me, speak to an integrity that exists only in nature. And I've become part of it. There's a wonderful epigram in Ray Grigg's *The Tao of Sailing*: "The wing of sail divides wind and then joins it together again. Nothing is used, so nothing is wasted. Nothing is taken, so nothing is returned. Nothing is done, yet things are not the same." I've never experienced quite this feeling on a rented sailboat, so indeed, things are not the same. Something has changed.

Patty is taking pictures from shore. I'm a couple hundred yards away now, beyond effective range of her small digital camera. It's time to turn around—to see if *Far From Perfect* will tack. Small, lightweight sailboats sometimes have trouble mustering enough momentum to turn the bow through the eye of the wind.

I push the tiller hard to starboard, and the boat obediently curls to port. The boom slowly drifts at me, lower than head level. It's at my shoulders. I practically lie down to let it pass overhead. When I pull myself up, we're on a beam reach again, but sailing in the opposite direction. A successful tack!

I sail the boat back to shore to collect Patty, and I realize I never lowered the centerboard to counteract the lateral force of the wind. In such a light breeze, it wasn't even needed. I've got to try it next to see if I can strike another item from the worry catalog: whether it'll pivot freely in its watertight sandwich. Patty boards, we shove off again, and as soon as we're in deep water I uncleat the lanyard that secures the centerboard. It's a three-foot length of polyester line.

The centerboard pivots exactly as it's supposed to.

I sputter an expletive that is grossly out of context on this lovely, tranquil lake.

"What happened?"

"I forgot to tie a figure-eight knot at the end of the lanyard. We've just lost it."

When the centerboard pivoted to its full "down" position, which is what we'd be using in a stiff wind, it pulled the lanyard with it, right through the hole in the cedar plank atop the centerboard trunk. The knot, had one existed, would have stopped it. Now the lanyard is jammed inside the narrow trunk, and the centerboard is stuck with it.

"Do you have anything in your toolbox to fish it out with?" Patty asks.

"I left my toolbox in the car."

I'm grateful for one thing: the churlish wisdom of not inviting any friends to witness this. It's not a disaster, but we're well into the fiasco spectrum. How can someone invest so much intimacy in a boat as I have with this one, then commit such a sequence of screwups in the first quarter-hour of actual operation? The only answer—and it has the tinny ring of an excuse—is that sailing is complicated, even on a dinghy, and newbies usually flounder until the moves become instinctive. Still, I *built* this thing.

"I guess we should go ahead and sail her for awhile, see if everything else works, then go ashore and try to retrieve the lanyard," I say. Patty agrees.

The wind doesn't cooperate. It dies, then resumes, then starts shifting direction every minute or two. This must be why I haven't seen anyone sailing on Beaver Lake: it's in a topographic bowl, and increasingly ringed with looming McMansions, so a light breeze encounters so many impediments that it's too shifty for good sailing. But *Far From Perfect* responds willingly, seems credibly stable, demonstrates no obvious vices except for the nuisance of the extremely low boom coming about. Joel Bergen told me he just catches his and lifts it over his head, so we'll try that.

After an hour, we sail and paddle her back to the launch, slowly grounding the centerboard on what I pray is a soft mud lakebed. There's a sickening *gggrrnnch!* that suggests it isn't. We crawl off the boat, getting immersed up to thighs—no great concern to Patty, since she's in her wetsuit—and I slog, dripping, a hundred yards to the car. There's nothing in my tool kit that can retrieve the centerboard lanyard, so I drive home for a coat hanger—this is growing more ignominious by the moment—while she waits with the boat.

The coat hanger doesn't work. The lanyard has somehow wedged itself very tightly beside the centerboard, which is thoroughly stuck.

We wrestle the boat halfway out of the water. I take the thin blade of the paddle and guide it into the trunk, then pound the paddle's other end with a hammer to try to unstick the centerboard. A fisherman on the shore twenty feet away glowers but doesn't say anything. I keep hammering and eventually move the board about six inches, but it's starting to splinter and the lanyard is still jammed. The final option appears to be to plunge under the boat and try to jerk the lanyard free from below. Which I would have done at the beginning if I'd been wearing my goddamn wetsuit.

From underneath, the lanyard pulls free surprisingly easily. Then I duct-tape it to a stiff wire, thread it back through its hole above, and tie the simple figure eight that it needed at the outset.

We cart the boat home. I scribble a list of eleven items that need attention, from a few spots of touch-up paint to a whole new arrangement for the seating. It's probably a good two weeks' worth of work. At that point, I'm scheduled to have a slightly more formal launch—in the bay behind Sam Devlin's shop.

"Can you save money by building a boat yourself, or is it actually more expensive this way?"

Far From Perfect is parked in the driveway, enjoying a day of welcome April sun while I reposition some of her hardware, and Ava, the precocious ten-year-old Bulgarian from across the street, is asking questions.

"That's kind of a devastating question, Ava," I say, hoping to derail the inquiry with a big word. It doesn't work—a hint of a knowing smile crosses her pixie face, and she just stands there, waiting. I stumble through a convoluted exposition that I end up not even understanding myself, and finally she wanders away.

It occurs to me that she's been observing my minuscule boat under construction from her upstairs bedroom window for one-seventh of her life, so it must seem to her that there's been some considerable expenditure here—in some form or another.

I've been keeping a ledger of both the money and hours I've spent on construction, so maybe this is the time to tally them and attempt a real answer to Ava's question. In the grownup world, of course, the part about "is it more expensive this way?" involves more than cash outlay, and I'll have to deal with some deeper issues. But first, let's just add numbers. I haven't checked myself, until now.

I seem to have spent a total of $4,175.73 on materials and supplies, including expendables such as sandpaper and solvents. This is 278 percent of my original wild-guess budget of $1,500, a cost-overrun proportion that's right up there in defense-contractor leagues. I spent another $966.32 on tools specifically for use on this project, and $108.55 getting the gift trailer licensed. So the total boat-related outlay so far has reached $5,250.60.

I've logged 419 hours of work spread across eighteen months. In his catalog blurb for the Zephyr plan, Sam Devlin breezily claims that "she can be built in just over 100 hours time." I'm at 400 percent of Sam's estimate, which is precisely in line with Mark Coté's "project rule."

I can see several ways to address Ava's question. We can strictly line up my $4,175 material costs with the most directly comparable production boat, the Crawford Melonseed, which at this writing lists for $8,900 plus shipping from New England. In this matchup, I save money.

But last September, prowling around Port Townsend's Wooden Boat Festival, Patty and I spotted a very pretty, fourteen-foot wooden daysailer in decent condition—she could have used some modest cosmetic improvements, but nothing major appeared amiss—for sale for $1,100. By that benchmark, my cash outlay alone on *Far From Perfect* looks idiotic.

If I value my time at $25 an hour, which I can manage writing and teaching when all the stars are aligned, I've invested $10,475 in labor. Adding the materials to that, I have, in theory, generated a pipsqueak boat of suspicious quality for $15,725. This is beyond absurd. Devlin himself would build it for less than that—I know; I asked. Around $11,000, he said. And Devlin's craftsmanship would be virtually perfect.

I'm having a hard time thinking of an honest answer to offer Ava, or any adult who's half as perceptive as she is, that isn't conflicted and overcomplicated. It would be terrific if I could claim that I've grown some useful skills or discipline from the work, but it's not clear that I have. My new abilities with a bandsaw would be useful only for building another, larger boat, which by definition would be more irrational than this one. The project has been fulfilling, but only in counterpoint with waves of doubt and discouragement.

From five yards away, or better yet, fifty, *Far From Perfect* is a heartbreakingly beautiful boat. The oak veneer on her deck catches the sun, strains it through an amber-and-chocolate sieve of wood grain, and rebroadcasts it as a soft, warm, organic glow. The sheer sweeps upward with a touch of insouciance, confidently proclaiming that her 1880 design is more than capable in 2010. (As if to confirm it, Joel Bergen just told me he'd taken his Zephyr out for a sail on Puget Sound, where a moderate breeze whipped her to a GPS-verified 5.5 knots—20 percent beyond what the physics textbook insists is her top speed.) The tanbark sail and varnished spruce mast sing tight, elegant harmonies with the cherry-red hull. Of course, when I get closer than five yards—as I must every morning when I squeeze by her starboard beam in the garage to deposit paper and plastic in the recycling bins—I'm irritated and disappointed. The failures are painfully apparent, especially the too-far-from-perfect epoxy finish on the deck. Up close, its waves and dimples scatter the garage light like a funhouse mirror.

I expect Sam will wince visibly—quiver and shake, even—when he inspects the deck. I'll promise him that I'll keep working on it.

But then there is deep beauty, the quality I've been contemplating for years, ever since that first wooden boat show. Regardless of her surface blemishes and imprecise fittings, there is an inner universe of beauty wrapped up in this little boat, not only in her physical essence but also in the process of her creation. And it isn't mystical or spiritual or theoretical, as I vaguely thought at the outset of The Year (and a Half) of the Boat. It's become real and tangible.

A few chapters back, I wrote that a sailboat—any sailboat—serves as a symbol of liberation. I still see it that way, but in a different and deeper sense. It isn't just about escaping the bonds of cell phones and Palm datebooks. It isn't about escape at all. It's a move *toward* finding a comfortable place at the intersection of technology and nature, one that's neither completely dependent on nor independent of the other.

The way I chose to build this boat doesn't repudiate technology. The bandsaw, random orbital sander, fiberglass and epoxy, and advice and commiseration via the Internet all contributed to making it a better boat than would have been possible at the time of the original nineteenth-century melonseeds. I'm almost certain I would have abandoned the project in midstream if I'd imposed an artificial historic overlay on it, eschewing electric tools and modern chemicals. But the end product, a simple sailboat that once underway uses no basic technology that wasn't available to Thoreau, embraces nature in a way that I think is profoundly beautiful.

Embracing nature isn't something out at the crackpot extreme of environmentalism. Think of it as a carpenter taking into account the grain of the wood, the way the fibers were naturally aligned as the tree grew, and fashioning an object so that the grain strengthens the piece instead of weakening it. If I had made the tiller so that the grain ran crosswise to the axis of stress, even someone with no experience in woodworking could see instinctively that it was wrong, and soon would come a disastrous crack to prove it. Like this, our web of ecological relationships can be realigned with the grain of the natural world, but it won't be easy: we'll be turning away from the dominion-over-all ethic that has its roots deep in the Old Testament. In the design and building of sailboats I discern a sweeping metaphor for cooperation with nature, and learning to sail has shown me that it need not feel like deprivation.

Another facet of deep beauty is the back story of the object at hand. The deeper the story, the richer the beauty. A factory-built sailboat slowly acquires a history of its owners' dreams, fears, and experiences—most good, a few terrifying—but it can hardly compare with a boat that *starts* its life on the water already full of its maker. Any handmade boat is an essay in values, and based on my experience, I would suspect that it had helped its builder to sort out and clarify those values in him- or herself. At best, it's a liberating experience, and *Far From Perfect* has been one. I think I'm significantly more patient, measurably more methodical, and slightly more courageous than I was on the day when Sam's plans arrived in the mail. I might be a little better at feeling at peace when I fall short of my own expectations; I've accepted that calibrated excellence is the best most of us can do. All these qualities are in the boat in approximate parallel with my character. Maybe others can't see them there, but I can, and they form a chart of how far I've come and how far I have to go.

On the surface, the reason for taking *Far From Perfect* to Olympia to show Sam is simply that he invited me to, almost a year back. But realistically, I doubt he remembers. He obviously has more businesslike things to do than entertain a stream of amateur builders trundling their imperfect efforts to his shop like sick puppies to a vet. At his expense, I seem to be answering some undefined internal need, something that won't accept validation without pushing against one last bit of resistance.

As the appointment approaches, I start to regret making it, and the anxiety mounts every day. The distraction of worry is contaminating the work I do on the boat in the meantime. On a couple of successive afternoons I take out one of the two crosswise thwarts and replace it with wider side-mounted seats that follow the curve of the hull sides. The new pieces end up with gaps between their ends and the hull ranging from zero to more than ⅛ of an inch. The chasms make no difference in terms of comfort or strength, but the work looks sloppy and I can't find the energy or even the desire to try to make it better. I'm in that zone Sam described with pinprick accuracy as "wanting the boat out of your life."

It's overcast and breezy when I roll into Sam's shop yard on a late April afternoon with *Far From Perfect* in tow. Probably too breezy for sailing, which will be a relief—I won't have to demonstrate my additional shortcomings on the water. Sam's in his office on the phone. As soon as he hangs up, he twists his big frame out of his chair. "Let's see her," he says, grinning and sounding as eager as a kid who's just been invited to look at dinosaur bones.

We walk outside. He stares at *Far From Perfect*'s port side for a long minute, then strides around to starboard. He kneels slightly to survey the hull's underside and skeg. Then he peers into the cockpit at the centerboard trunk and the mast and boom bungeed down for transport. He feels underneath the deck, finding the lumberyard quarter-round trim I used to brace the coaming, which wasn't in the plans. I feel an urgent need to fill the silence with something. I have an elaborate apologia that I mentally rehearsed on the drive to Olympia.

"Cool!" he barks, just as I'm about to launch my much less laudatory appraisal. "You made a really nice boat. This is the first Zephyr I've seen, and I've really been wondering what it would look like."

"You've never built one yourself?" I ask.

"No," he says, sounding slightly sheepish. "I probably should, though."

The tension evaporates, and we spend the next hour poking and prodding the details. He doesn't mind that I left out the deck brace; he thinks the miscellaneous reinforcements I arranged under the deck will cover for it. He tells me to quit worrying about the transom. He likes my improvised seats. He doesn't mention the mismatched grain of the stem or the little kinks in the hull curvature caused by my two-piece sheer clamps. The one serious shortcoming he finds is the rudder, which I made out of ½-inch okoume. He says the stress of holding the boat on course against weather could break it, which would constitute a real emergency in a big wind. I figure it's another brain fart on my part, like overlooking the deck brace, but when we check the Zephyr's materials list it specifies either ¾-inch hardwood *or* ½-inch plywood. Finally seeing a Zephyr in the flesh, Sam's eye tells him the plywood is too flimsy. Who am I to argue? I'll rebuild it—the rudder is one of the few parts I haven't yet made twice.

"You notice the deck bulge, like there's a Corvette engine under the hood," I say.

"It was actually the first thing I noticed," he says. "Were the bulkhead dimensions wrong on the plans?"

"No. I just made a bunch of little mistakes, and they compounded into a big one."

"The best way to deal with a mistake like this is to call attention to it, and then it disappears," he says. "It's counterintuitive, but it works." He takes the boat's profile rendering on the plan and sketches a wooden cockscomb two or three inches high that would stream back from the bow along the misshapen deck to the mast—an accoutrement so unusual that no one, in theory, would then notice the hump underneath it. It could be made functional with a cleat for tying off the sprit snotter, making it easier to adjust the sprit underway.

"Of course you can see that the epoxy finish on the deck is pretty uneven," I say. "I can do better, and I'm going to spend the summer on it. It's just a matter of buckling down to the grind."

"I wouldn't bother," he says. "It's really not important."

"I don't know how you can say that—the brightwork on your boats looks like Scandinavian furniture."

"Well, as you've learned, you can work on these things forever. There's no end to how far you can take it. The place we stop is the place where it's better than what we did on the boat just before."

He asks me if there's anything in the plans that ought to be changed. I'm surprised by the question—there's a presumption in it that I actually know something about boatbuilding. It suddenly occurs to me that I've built one more Zephyr than Sam has. And in fact, I do have a couple of suggestions. I crudely sketch the easier ways I figured out to build the mast step into the hull and attach the coaming to the deck. "What I did wasn't the way you'd do it, given your boatbuilding skills," I say. "I just devised things that seemed more accessible to an amateur."

"I agree," Sam says.

After we finish dissecting the details, he asks about the big picture—how I felt about the boatbuilding experience. I tell him that first, there was quite a bit more of it than I had expected. "You advertise 'just over 100 hours,' in the plans catalog." I say. "I logged 419 hours before the first launch, and the clock's still running."

He laughs, not apologetically. "I had to put *some* number in there. I'm actually less of a liar than a lot of designers. There's a famous plan for a 'six-hour canoe' out there. I've seen a lot with sixty hours in them."

I tell him then that it was a character-building experience, and that it has enriched my life in ways that are yet to fully play out. It doesn't seem like the right time or place to talk about the cycles of self-doubt and discouragement. He seems to want to make this into the ceremony I had denied myself, only a private one, without the crowd and champagne-drenched launching. He asks me to sign a photo of *Far From Perfect* for him to keep. As I do it, I find my eyes becoming moist and my throat tightening. I can't believe I'm having to fight back tears. I don't cry, ever. Not my style. I look away so he won't see my eyes.

"You're a boatbuilder now," he says. "You're entitled to wear the boatbuilder shoes, boatbuilder pants, boatbuilder jacket. This wasn't a kit. I don't mean to denigrate that process, but that's just assembly. This is taking a pile of wood and breathing life into it. For us as men, I think this is the closest we can come to giving birth. This is as creative as we can possibly be."

I remind him that I named my creation *Far From Perfect* and that it richly deserves the name. I'm still trying to deflect undeserved praise. But Sam doesn't seem to care how imperfectly his design was realized. The simple fact that the birth occurred is miracle enough to make him happy.

"I love the name," he laughs.

The only thing left to do today is talk about the next boat. Most of the people who buy a Devlin plan and actually complete a boat—he estimates the success rate may be as high as 40 or 50 percent—have a *next* boat in their dreams. Bigger and more ambitious, it goes without saying. I tell him I'd like to buy the study plans for his Winter Wren, a nineteen-foot, gaff-rigged sloop that I've been sneaking periodic looks at in his online catalog. He fetches the plans and refuses my fifteen bucks.

"Save it for your pile of wood," he says.

THE TEACHINGS OF
A WOODEN SAILBOAT

FAR FROM PERFECT IS IN her place at the September Wooden Boat Festival in Port Townsend, docked demurely between a fifteen-foot Devlin Nancy's China and a twenty-five-foot Folkboat. More than two hundred boats have crowded into this year's show, ranging from the breathtaking one-hundred-year-old schooner *Martha* to a sixty-pound sailing canoe. The atmosphere is pure festival, a celebration of the rediscovered splendor of wooden boats. There's no competition, and none of the snooty hauteur you'd find at a concours d'élégance of classic cars. Although some of the boats represent serious money, an unspoken egalitarianism seems to embrace all of us participating in the show. Building or maintaining a wooden boat takes hard work, dedication, and occasional ingenuity; it has no correspondence to social class or formal education.

I had spent the summer slowly improving *Far From Perfect*: an entirely new rudder, better rigging, stronger brackets for the removable rowing seat on top of the centerboard trunk. Against Sam's advice, I invested ten days in trying to smooth out the deck with a new round of epoxy and five more coats of varnish. It yielded maybe a 50 percent improvement, which seemed well worth the trouble. And now at the festival, *Far From Perfect* has been favored with a happy accident of celestial geography: the southerly arc of the September sun is preventing dockside viewers from seeing the direct reflection that would reveal how imperfect the finish remains. From comments I overhear, people seem to think she's rather fetching, and they're charmed by her name. "*Far From Perfect*—ought to be the name of everything I own," one man said. When they ask, I tell them the name was the smartest move I made in the entire construction process—it relieved a lot of pressure. They get it.

The dumbest move now appears to be one I made a week ago in last-minute preparations for Port Townsend: I defaced the deck with two-dollar plastic horn cleats to tie on dock lines and fenders. Several more festoon the mast. When the boat was alone in the garage, or even at this book's cover photo shoot at a lake, they'd seemed like a reasonable choice—honest, functional, and unpretentious, like the Zephyr design itself. But in the context of the festival, a sweeping celebration of craftsmanship, they now look inexcusably cheesy. They're functioning perfectly well, but contradicting the spirit of the whole wooden boat revival. I wander through the forest of boats and fail to find *any* mass-produced plastic in such prominent use.

There's a small bronze foundry with a display of its boat hardware at the festival. I wander over to inquire about their cleats—I'm thinking of slipping back into the marina in the evening with my drill after the crowds have dispersed and prematurely retiring the plastic. Twenty-six bucks apiece, the bronze man says. The boat has twelve cleats. No, this isn't the solution.

I vaguely recall clipping and filing an old article about how to *make* wooden cleats with a bandsaw, so I shamble over to the Edensaw Hardwoods tent to ask the experts what kind of wood would be hard and tough enough. Purpleheart, they tell me, and for twenty bucks I can buy enough to fabricate a whole boatload of cleats. Of course, the same qualities that make purpleheart strong enough to do the work of a cleat will make it fiercely resistant to being shaped into a cleat, so I'm looking at several weeks of labor to replace my perfectly serviceable plastic.

Is this reasonable? There's no universal answer, no absolute right or wrong. It depends on the boat, the owner, and what they intend to do together. It is a question of values, which is more a spiritual issue than a practical one. And this is what building a wooden boat does for you: It becomes an ongoing workshop in clarifying values, sifting through the options, and making the best decisions. Through practice on the infinitesimal, irrelevant-to-the-rest-of-the-world issues of whether to craft a bunch of four-inch cleats by hand, or make another run at an improved finish on the deck, or ponder the temptation to tack on swoopy but nonfunctional flying buttresses, you build up the moral muscles for making the big decisions: the ones that affect other human lives, or the quality of life on earth.

It doesn't have to be a boat. Another person's *Far From Perfect* could be a cabin in the woods, a bluegrass band, a new career, or teaching sustainable agriculture in Nicaragua. Many of the underlying questions of values and applications of principle will be remarkably similar. There will be the same struggle to reconcile the ideal with the possible, and the same tension between discipline and creative flexibility. If it's a life-changing project, it will require at least as much perseverance as the building of a wooden boat. In the end you are likely to emerge with more humility than pride (unless you can name your boat/cabin/band *Perfection*, with justification), and that is a good thing. You are also likely to have created something that adds a speck of joy or beauty to the world.

I'd like to take a couple of final pages here to lay out the most useful principles I learned, practical and philosophical, from my work on *Far From Perfect*. They aren't only about boatbuilding. Apply that flexibility of mind, and you may see how they can affect any endeavor for the better. Of course they don't guarantee success. But they are at least the building blocks of a more fulfilling adventure.

When contemplating this adventure, take a sheet of paper and draw a couple of bars, or goal markers, on opposite sides. The left bar represents something you know you can do successfully. In my case, I could have easily built a small sailboat from a kit. The right bar is an accomplishment that would be phenomenal, Herculean, the all-but-impossible forty-foot schooner. A minuscule minority of the highly gifted and driven should rightly aim for that goal on the right. For the rest of us, the reasonable route is something in between.

Buy the best tools or instruments you can find, even when they seem like an extravagance at the point of purchase. Cheap tools are short-lived, frustrating, often incompetent, and occasionally even dangerous. They do not inspire respect, and a craftsperson who does not respect his or her tools is not on the way to creating durable and beautiful things with them. Good tools form an investment of belief in yourself, and while you're learning a craft, they will be more forgiving of poor technique. A tool that is better than you are will encourage you to grow into it and will absorb a shared history of craftsmanship with you as the years and decades pass.

Train yourself to anticipate problems and devise solutions before they occur, like the little mast-securing line Joel Bergen installed on *Quality Time*. This isn't the same thing as expecting the worst; it's visualizing how events might unfold and being prepared to deal with all the possibilities.

At the end of today's work, stop at a point where you know what the next step will be when you resume tomorrow. If you don't know where you're going next, you're liable to wake up at 3 a.m. and worry about it, or resist resuming at all. Knowing where you're going and being primed to tackle the first ten minutes of the job preserves momentum, which is precious capital. Writer Annie Dillard describes her relationship with a book-in-progress as like keeping a barely domesticated beast in the study that can turn feral overnight. "You must visit it every day and reassert your mastery over it. If you skip a day, you are, quite rightly, afraid to open the door to its room." So it is with a boat, a painting, your tax return, or any other creative endeavor.

Despite the value of momentum, there are times when you just shouldn't work on anything you seriously care about. These conditions may differ for you, but for me the no-work emotional zones are times when I'm angry, resentful, frustrated, fatigued, or impatient. During these cycles I can either perform a half hour of token work on the boat, something like sanding or paint masking that requires no great skill, or go rake leaves. If I approach my boat with a drill in my hand and resentment in my head, I'm going to build that temper into the boat—and then have to spend hours undoing the damage, which will only stoke more resentment. Thus, what should be a fulfilling experience turns into a miserable one, and an unfinished boat gets chainsawed into firewood.

There is a substantial difference between striving for excellence and striving for perfection, and much of the struggle involved in your endeavor will be to understand and come to terms with that difference. It will help to remember that if you're doing it for yourself, you alone are entitled to define "excellence."

Don't be too proud to ask for help. In the boatbuilding world there is almost no problem that someone hasn't faced and licked before, and Internet forums have made it easy to connect with expertise worldwide. In my experience, it's always given gracefully and respectfully if requested in like manner. Through such connections we create community, an endlessly widening ripple out of the personal act of creation.

Ultimately, however, you have to do what feels right to you, even if an expert advises against it. In most cases you will simply learn the reason why the expert pointed another way, and toss your mistake in the sprawling pile of junk under the boat. But occasionally you will discover something, perhaps something useful or beautiful, something never seen or done before on earth.

GLOSSARY

I loathe jargon, and the boat world employs more of it than any other field I can think of, including law. But much of it is unavoidable—there are innumerable specialized parts and functions on a boat, and they all need names. I tried to define uncommon words whenever they spilled into the story, but for easy reference, here's an orderly (though informal) glossary.

Bowsprit A spar projecting forward off the bow of a sailboat, providing an attachment point for a larger jib than could be attached at the bow.

Chine The intersection of a hull where the sides meet the bottom pieces.

Coaming A raised wooden framework around a cockpit.

Dinghy A small boat usually powered by sails or oars.

Dory A small, flat-bottomed rowboat.

Draft The depth of water needed to float a boat or ship.

Forestay A sturdy wire that leads from the top of the mast to the bow, securing the mast and providing an attachment for a jib.

Gunwale The top edge of the side of the hull.

Jib A triangular sail set in front of the main or forward mast.

Jibe To turn a boat running downwind so that the wind drives the sail from the opposite side of the boat (also spelled *gybe*).

Keel A fin-like projection extending down from the centerline of the hull, essential to prevent sideways drift (leeway) on a sailboat.

Knot One nautical mile per hour, equal to 1.15 miles per hour.

Mast step A sturdy wooden block or framework in the hull that receives the heel of the mast.

Pram A small sailboat or rowboat, usually with a snub-nose bow.

Sheer The uppermost line of the hull in profile view.

Sheet A line (rope) that controls the position of a sail.

Skeg A fin attached to the after end of a boat's hull. In contrast to a keel, a skeg's main function is to help a boat track in a straight line.

Sloop A sailboat with a single mast and two sails, a mainsail and jib.

Stem The piece of a boat's frame at the leading edge of the bow; one of the important "bones" of its structure.

Tack To turn the bow of a sailboat through the eye of the wind so that the boat changes heading at least 90 degrees and the wind drives the sail from the opposite side of the boat.

Transom The back, or aft, wall of the hull.

References and Resources

If you're now thinking you might—just might—want to consider building a boat, there are many easily obtainable resources that will help you get educated and start moving.

Greg Rössel's *The Boatbuilder's Apprentice* offers a clear and comprehensive overview of five distinct methods of building wooden boats. If you already know you want to build a leakproof wood-and-fiberglass composite boat using the stitch-and-glue technique, Samual Devlin's own book, *Devlin's Boatbuilding*, is indispensable. The online *WoodenBoat* Store at www.woodenboatstore.com carries an enormous selection of books, videos, plans, models, and coffee mugs. It won't hurt to spend a few bucks on purely inspirational material, so order Benjamin Mendlowitz's spectacular *Calendar of Wooden Boats*, which has been coming out annually for more than a quarter-century.

It's a good idea to buy an inexpensive study plan first for any boat you're considering, because complete construction plans for small boats typically cost anywhere from $50 to $250. Study plans usually run about $15. Besides the *WoodenBoat* Store, some of the best sources for plans are Glen-L Marine Designs at www.boatdesigns.com; Selway Fisher Design at www.selway-fisher.com; and Devlin at www.devlinboat.com. (Also check out Sam Devlin's custom design website at www.samdevlin.com.) Duckworks online magazine has an omnibus link page to dozens of plan suppliers, www.duckworksmagazine.com. A dangerous seduction lurking in all these online plans catalogs is photos of many of the amateur-built boats constructed from them.

These amateur builders themselves form a vast international pool of information. You'll be able to contact some of them via online links from the plans catalogs or find them through Google. You can also go to one of the many annual wooden boat gatherings and ask questions (and rub up to the lovely boats) in person. Two of the largest are the Wooden Boat Festival in Port Townsend, Washington; and the Wooden Boat Show in Mystic, Connecticut.

There are too many web-based boatbuilders' forums and blogs to list here, but they're easy to find with a search engine, and there's a wealth of information in them. Peter Gron's meticulously illustrated blog on the building of his Arctic Tern is phenomenal. Its address may have changed by the time this book appears in print, but Peter promised we'll always be able to locate it by searching his name. There are also several print magazines that are very useful to boaters, builders, and dreamers. *WoodenBoat* magazine is the best known, but check out *Small Craft Advisor* as well.

With all the technology and information so easily at hand, there's never been a better time to build a wooden boat.

Appreciation

My first and deepest thanks must go to my wife, Patty Cheek, whose faith and encouragement never wavered. Even when she would accompany me to the marine supply store and watch yet another bill for premium epoxy and arcane boat hardware top $300, she would only flinch—not groan or wail.

Several boatbuilders, amateur and professional, very generously provided time, information, and when I finally forced myself to ask for it, advice. They also became friends, and I'm grateful for that, too: Vicki Altizer, Joel Bergen, Sam Devlin, Joe Greenley, and Peter Gron. Paddling buddy Howard Greene, classic wooden boat maven Mike Murray, Windworks CEO Greg Norwine, and lawyer/artist Bill Weissinger belong here, also.

Many neighbors and friends graciously gave a hand with the boat, helping with everything from lifting and moving to sanding and filling, incredibly. They include Nick Bannon, Mark Coté, Merrill Grant, David Israel, Ivan Trindev and Elena Trindeva, Ron Wahlin, George and Pam Whitehouse, Elizabeth Whitehouse, and Lynn Wood.

And still more good friends—most of these are fellow writers—read various parts of the book and provided valuable encouragement and advice. They are Steve Blakeslee, Deb Caletti, Deborah Folka, Curt Gustafson, Susan Hazen-Hammond, Jane Isenberg, Susan Jensen, Dennis Ryerson, Les Wallach, and Joyce Yarrow.

An astonished thanks goes to Dr. Doug Lee, who *gave* us his perfectly good boat trailer.

The amazing library at Seattle's Center for Wooden Boats offered a rich trove of resources for researching the history of boatbuilding and sailing. Both CWB's Lake Union Wooden Boat Festival and the Port Townsend Wooden Boat Festival provided inspiration and impossibly high standards to strive for. Finally, I especially appreciate Greg and Nina Dortch, owners of the excellent Holly Hill House B&B in Port Townsend. Quite a bit of this book was drafted in their Victorian living room during my frequent expeditions to Port Townsend, and the writing just seemed to happen more smoothly there.

About the Author

Lawrence W. Cheek has written fifteen nonfiction books on travel, architecture, nature, and prehistoric North America. He currently teaches nonfiction writing at the University of Washington and works as architecture critic for the *Seattle Post-Intelligencer*. He divides his too-scarce free time among sailing, sea kayaking, hiking, and boatbuilding.